REPERTOIRE

REPERTOIRE

THE BEST VEGETARIAN RECIPES TO
BUILD A MODERN COOK'S COLLECTION

Alice Hart

For James

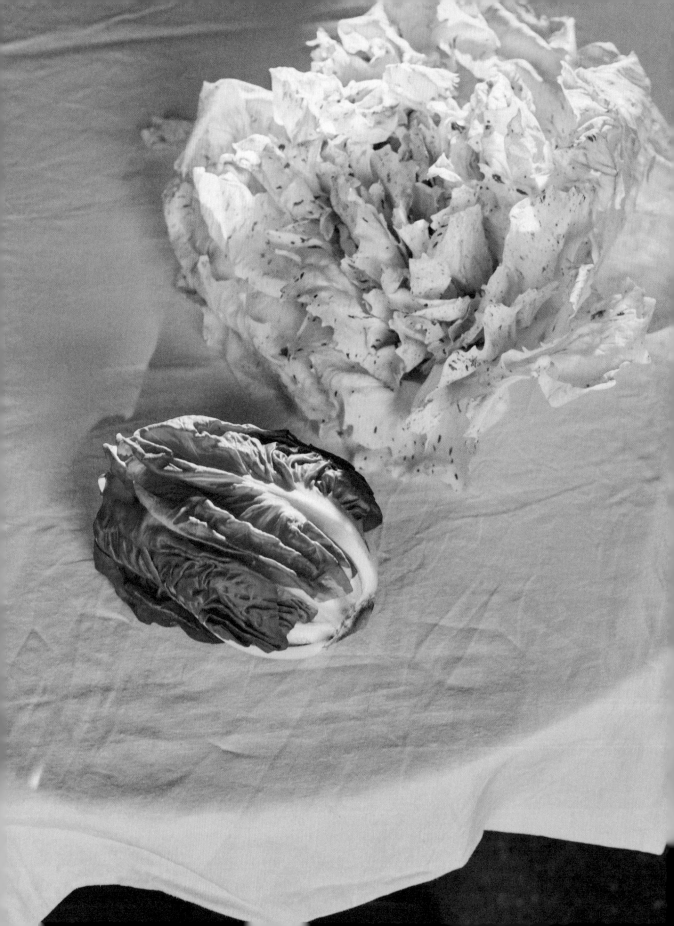

CONTENTS

INTRODUCTION

This is a book of greatest hits, designed to be the ultimate vegetarian book for your kitchen: a complete repertoire of modern classics, future classics and 'signature' dishes for every occasion.

Vegetarian cookery, for me, is first, foremost and always a celebration of vegetables. The landscape of vegetarian cookery has expanded and evolved since I wrote my first vegetarian and vegan book but I have remained true to my ethos as a cook, writer and nutritionist. Seasonal, colourful vegetables, treated with care and balance, form the bedrock of every recipe. From there, the occasion, the mood, the time or motivation available, the appetite for spice or calm as well as the appetite for sustenance can all follow in turn, but we always begin with the vegetables, fruits, herbs, wholegrains and spices at hand.

All this is to say, while I adore a clever shortcut and pass on many chefs' tricks so you may prep ahead and better enjoy the process of creating dishes, you simply won't find processed meat pretenders on these pages. It isn't my style. You'll find what I deem to be 'real' food, intended to be a pleasure to cook as well as eat and truly designed for everyone, whether they only eat in a plant-based way or sit somewhere along the spectrum of flexitarian. Maybe you have a vegetarian loved one to cook for? Perhaps you adore vegetables and flavour as part of a largely omnivorous diet and are looking for ideas to accompany your Sunday roast or barbecue. You'll find inspiration and encouragement here.

The question of what to cook as a vegetarian or for vegetarians rings as loudly as it did nearly 20 years ago when I wrote my first book. Of course, there is privilege at play when emphasising how much choice there is for the home cook; how the vast array of seasonal produce at hand is the only inspiration you need. Assumptions are being made about herbs, spices, vegetables, salads, legumes and pulses, nuts and seeds, good oils, fruits and wholegrains being available to you, the reader. But cooking real food in this way is the best value, most nutritionally dense and most enjoyable way to eat that I know of.

Gravitating towards fresh, vibrant flavours often translates as a celebration of world cuisines where vegetables are king. I'm the first to admit that, though heavily inspired by and adoring of, say, Thai or South Indian flavours, I do sometimes adapt cooking methods or ingredients from those regions to suit what is commonly available in Western kitchens. I hope my adaptations – and my borrowings of those beloved flavours – have been respectful and humble. Our enlightened palates know the sting of chilli, the satisfaction of a balanced dressing, the quiet impact of an elegant risotto and have come to expect that variety and pleasure. Be brave with your cooking! You are allowed to be curious, to experiment with unfamiliar ingredients and to fall in love with them. Where I've taken the liberty of altering or adapting a 'classic', it is with the intention of updating it to suit current tastes and lifestyles, not to imply it required bettering. I've striven to write a vegetarian love letter to bold, global flavours.

Dairy can be an elephant in the modern vegetarian kitchen. You'll find characterful, good-quality cheeses on these pages, but I use them with enormous care, for texture and flavour and not merely for the sake of it. There are generous amounts of cool, sharp yogurt and labneh here too, but I find little need for too much in the way of cream or rich sauces in savoury dishes. Please buy the very best quality you can afford when purchasing dairy and free-range eggs, and I mean that with animal welfare in mind as much as I do flavour. Adapt as you will to make recipes vegan friendly. Many of these recipes are vegan anyway or you'll often find you can leave out an ancillary dairy component.

We begin this book in the morning, with breakfast, brunch and lunch. In reality, these are movable feasts. Who hasn't enjoyed brunch-style food in the evening when a proper supper isn't needed? A chapter of small plates follows, running the gamut from party snack to dip to starter to light meal. The supper recipes are geared towards gatherings and larger appetites. Then, a collection of side recipes that are anything but accessories; every single one can be adapted or built on to make the basis of a meal. I wanted to remind you there was more to side vegetables than steamed broccoli and to inspire everyone to add more vegetable dishes to their meals, whether they habitually eat in a plant-based way or not.

Gutsy, satisfying flavours are an undeniable theme of this book. To really get the point across, there is an entire chapter dedicated to sauces – entitled The Sauce. It's a gift of pickles, spice mixes, dressings, ferments and pestos that will add true oomph to your kitchen. They can stand alone but are also woven throughout the recipes in the book as suggested condiments and additions. A confident and indulgent desserts chapter rounds us off in style. This is a sociable compilation of vegetarian recipes, suitable for feasting and every day, so a collection of puddings and sweet treats was called for.

I have often used the definite article in this book, either to describe a carefully honed adaption of a well-loved recipe – an 'ultimate' or definitive interpretation for the vegetarian repertoire, as it were – or to title a chapter with the gravitas such a grouping deserves. A little grandeur is called for when deciding what constitutes a recipe fit for a repertoire.

Every cookery writer must aspire for their book to be heavily thumbed and sauce-spattered, imagining it sitting on the side in a kitchen, consulted often or flicked through for inspiration. That's certainly how I've imagined this book: one to use and use again.

BRUNCH, LUNCH

You'll find savoury starts in this chapter, for the most part, with a couple of fruit-based breakfasts thrown in to balance and expand your morning repertoire. Apart from the sweet options, I'd warrant every other recipe could stand in for lunch, or even a laid-back supper, so I've tried to encourage that in the title. If you prefer timid flavours to start the day, you'll certainly want to push them back anyway; there are bold flavours at play here and some unconventional offerings. The idea of, say, a Green Lentil & Pea Dhal, thrumming with chilli and turmeric, for brunch might be too much for some palates, but beyond that – and I'm writing with those who like to start the day with bread or cereal in mind here – there's no reason we shouldn't throw convention out of the window in favour of starting the day with vegetables and spice. It works for much of the planet.

Do I need to clarify that these are most likely to be weekend or holiday recipes if you intend to make them in the morning? Hence not calling them breakfast. If you have the time or the lifestyle, by all means make them first thing on any day, but I would expect a stack of Ricotta Hotcakes with Spiced Honey & Raspberries to become a lazy Sunday tradition and a Winter Tomato Confit with Tahini, Sage & Chickpeas to be a rather special lunch.

Inevitably, given its partial brunch theme, this chapter showcases eggs more than any other. I make no apologies for giving you plenty of ideas. If you love them and eat them, eggs are an incredibly useful and good-quality source of protein for vegetarians. I try not to veer too far into nutrition-speak in cookery books – in spite of my nutritionist credentials – feeling it better to let enticing, colourful (and yes, nutritious) recipes do the talking – carrot over stick, as it were – but a Lentil & Spinach Shakshuka, mini Greens & Chilli Frittatas stuffed with green veg and chilli and a sweet-sour muddle of Agrodolce Peppers with Capers & Sourdough make wonderful protein-rich meals at any time of the day. You could also add a fried or poached egg or two to the dhal, The Ultimate Avocado Toast or the Miso & Charred Greens Bowl.

THE ULTIMATE AVOCADO TOAST

A vibrant and totally OTT version of an old faithful, resplendent with lime-spiked avocado, smoky black beans, chilli oil and pickles. Add poached eggs, if you like, or forget about both those and the feta to create a vegan version. This recipe calls for the Pink Pickles. If you don't have any, make a cheat's version by tossing a finely sliced red onion or two large shallots with a dash of red wine vinegar, a large pinch of sugar and a pinch of salt. Set aside for 20 minutes, stirring now and then. They will be pickled enough. Drain and use as below. Again, use your favourite bought crisp chilli oil if you haven't made the Fragrant Chilli Oil.

Serves 4
Preparation time: 25 minutes
Cooking time: 12 minutes

3 garlic cloves
1 banana shallot (echalion), finely chopped
4 tbsp extra virgin olive oil
1–2 tsp chipotle chilli paste, to taste
1 tsp hot smoked paprika
1 tsp finely chopped oregano
400g (14oz) tin of black beans, rinsed and drained
2 large limes, juice of 1½, remaining half in wedges
3 large, ripe avocados, halved and stoned
a handful of coriander (cilantro) leaves, finely chopped
4 large, thick slices of sourdough bread
4 heaped tbsp Pink Pickles (page 168), drained
4 tsp Fragrant Chilli Oil (page 172) or ready-made chilli oil
100g (3½oz) feta, drained and crumbled
a pinch of dried chilli (hot pepper) flakes (optional)
sea salt and freshly ground black pepper
a large handful of sprouts, shoots or salad leaves, to serve

Set aside half a garlic clove, then crush the remainder.

To make the smoky beans, put a small frying pan (skillet) over a low heat. Add the shallot and 2 tablespoons of the olive oil and allow to soften for 6 minutes or so, stirring until translucent and sweet. Add the crushed garlic, chipotle (2 teaspoons if you like it hot), paprika and oregano. Cook for a minute, then stir in the beans with a splash of water, increase the heat to medium and continue to cook down until the spices are cooked out and become fragrant, stirring almost constantly. Season with salt and pepper, taste and adjust with a few drops of lime juice, if needed. The finished beans should be dry and not sauce-y. Set aside.

Scoop the avocado flesh from the skins into a bowl and roughly crush to your desired texture with the remaining lime juice, the coriander and salt and pepper to taste.

Griddle or toast the bread until charred, then rub all over with the cut side of the remaining half garlic clove. Drizzle the uppermost sides with the remaining olive oil and scatter with a little salt.

Spoon or spread the avocado mixture over the toast and top with a scattering of smoky beans, the pink pickles, chilli oil, feta, extra dried chilli flakes, if liked, and plenty of black pepper. Accompany each plate with a small wedge of lime for squeezing and a sprightly handful of sprouts, shoots or salad leaves.

CHIPOTLE HUEVOS RANCHEROS

The whole works and such a winning version of a classic. Making a fresh tomato sauce – using the oven to concentrate flavours with ease – makes a world of difference and can be done a day or two ahead of time. The refried beans can also be made a day or so ahead. Even so, I've kept this as a dish for two as frying more than four eggs to order is a faff. You'll find chilli in adobo in little cans in specialist delis or online. Substitute each whole chilli in sauce with a teaspoon of chipotle chilli paste from a little jar if the latter is more readily available where you live.

Serves 2
Preparation time: 20 minutes
Cooking time: 50 minutes

1 sweet white onion, thickly sliced
500g (1lb 2oz) plum tomatoes,
    thickly sliced
1 red chilli, roughly sliced
4 tbsp olive oil
1 chipotle chilli in adobo or 2 tsp
    chipotle chilli paste
a small bunch of coriander
    (cilantro), leaves and stalks
    roughly chopped separately
1 tsp cumin seeds
1 tsp hot smoked paprika
1 garlic clove, crushed
400g (14oz) tin of borlotti beans,
    drained and liquid reserved
2 limes, 1 juiced, 1 halved
4 very fresh eggs
4 corn tortillas, 10–12cm
    (4–4½in) diameter
1 ripe avocado, halved, stoned and
    roughly chopped
hot sauce or dried chipotle chilli (hot
    pepper) flakes, to serve (optional)
sea salt and freshly ground
    black pepper

Preheat the oven to 200°C fan (220°C/425°F/gas 7).

To make the sauce, put the onion, tomatoes and chilli in a large roasting tin, season with salt and pepper and drizzle with 2 tablespoons of olive oil. Roast for 30 minutes until browned and sizzling. Ideally, for the best texture, tip into a food processor with the chipotle chilli and coriander stalks. Pulse to chop into a rough sauce, then transfer to a saucepan. Alternatively, tip the roasting tin contents and chipotle stalks straight into a wide saucepan, using a hand-held blender to break the mixture down. Either way, the sauce shouldn't be overly smooth. Taste and add a little more seasoning if needed; it should be both fresh and sonorous.

To make the refried beans, put ½ tablespoon of the oil in a small, cold saucepan with the cumin seeds, paprika and garlic. Place over a low heat and cook gently for a few minutes until the garlic begins to sizzle but not colour. Add the drained beans with a generous twist of salt and pepper and cook for a couple of minutes, stirring. Add 3–4 tablespoons of the bean liquid from the tin, heat through for 30 seconds, then squeeze in the lime juice, add most of the chopped coriander leaves and mash down roughly with the back of a spoon. Keep warm.

Put a tablespoon of oil in a large, non-stick frying pan (skillet) set over a medium heat and crack in the eggs, spacing them out well. Fry gently, flicking the hot oil over the whites with a spoon every now and then until they look opaque and crisp at the edges. They should take 3–4 minutes but cook them for longer if you prefer a firmer yolk. Transfer to a warm plate.

Return the pan to the heat with the remaining oil, turn the heat up a notch and fry the tortillas for 1–2 minutes on each side until crisp and beginning to brown. Transfer to a plate lined with paper towels to absorb any excess oil.

Transfer the tortillas to serving plates, nestle the eggs on top and cloak with the tomato sauce. Accompany with the beans, avocado and the lime halves to squeeze over. Scatter with a few coriander leaves to finish and consider peppering with hot sauce or a dusting of dried chipotle chilli flakes, if liked.

WINTER TOMATO CONFIT
WITH TAHINI, SAGE & CHICKPEAS

The magic of this plate will rest on the tomatoes you choose. Though a stint in the oven with good olive oil and garlic will tease flavour out of insipid tomatoes, if you start with something special – larger heritage varieties for preference – you'll end up with a heavenly, syrupy confit to spoon over a sesame yogurt with spiced chickpeas. Simple and chic.

Serves 4 as starter or small plate
Preparation time: 20 minutes
Cooking time: 50 minutes

800g (1lb 12oz) large heritage
   tomatoes, halved horizontally
5 large garlic cloves, unpeeled
   and whole
6 tbsp extra virgin olive oil, plus extra
   to drizzle
finely grated zest and juice of 1 lemon
400g (14oz) tin of chickpeas
   (garbanzos), rinsed and drained
1½ tsp sweet paprika
½ tsp chilli (hot pepper) flakes
1 tsp cumin seeds
about 16 small sage leaves
200g (7oz/generous ¾ cup) strained
   Greek yogurt
1 tbsp tahini
4–8 long slices of rustic baguette
2 tbsp Dukkah (page 183) or
   ready-made
sea salt and freshly ground
   black pepper

Preheat the oven to 170°C fan (190°C/375°F/gas 5).

Place the halved tomatoes in a roasting tin and nestle 4 of the garlic cloves in between. Drizzle with about 4 tablespoons of the olive oil and roast for about 50 minutes, or until the tomatoes are reduced, shrivelled and almost collapsing. Season with half the lemon juice. Remove the garlic cloves from their skins, returning them to the pan, and set aside.

Meanwhile, toss the chickpeas with a further 2 tablespoons of oil, the lemon zest, paprika, chilli flakes and cumin seeds in a bowl. Season well with salt and pepper, tip onto a baking sheet and roast for 15 minutes. Toss the sage leaves through and return to the oven for a further 10 minutes until golden and crisp.

Combine the yogurt, tahini and remaining lemon juice in a bowl. Crush half the remaining garlic clove, stir into the yogurt and season to taste with salt and pepper. Toast a couple of slices of baguette per person, then rub with the cut side of the remaining half garlic clove, drizzle with extra virgin olive oil and salt lightly.

To serve, place the warm tomatoes on a base of the tahini yogurt, spooning any syrupy juices from the pan over the top. Drizzle with extra virgin olive oil, then scatter with the roast chickpeas and the dukkah. Nestle the slices of hot, toasted bread alongside to dip.

APPLE, AMSTERDAM &
PICKLED WALNUT TOASTED SANDWICHES

A sublime toastie – indulgent, perhaps, but perfectly balanced and singing with flavour. Make this as an autumnal brunch, snack or supper, served with extra rocket on the side in the latter case.

Makes 2
Preparation time: 15 minutes
Cooking time: 10 minutes

150g (5oz) Old Amsterdam or other mature, characterful Gouda, rind removed

1 large eating (dessert) apple, such as Pink Lady, cored

30g (1oz) salted butter, softened

4 slices of thick wholemeal, rye or seeded bread

4 tbsp Summer Herb & Seed Pesto (page 175) or ready-made fresh pesto

100g (3½oz) drained pickled walnuts, sliced

a handful of wild rocket (arugula) leaves, plus extra to serve

Cut the cheese into 5mm (¼in) thick slices. Thinly slice the apple. I find it easiest to do this horizontally in rounds. Eat the top and bottom pieces, reserving the neat, whole slices.

Butter one side of all 4 bread slices and place them on a chopping board in pairs, buttered-sides down. Evenly spread all four slices of bread with pesto – this is to 'glue' the other ingredients in place more effectively. Top 2 pesto-ed slices with half the sliced cheese in an even layer. Top this with the pickled walnuts, rocket leaves and overlapping apple slices. Finish with the rest of the sliced cheese, as evenly as possible, and flip the remaining pesto-spread slices on top, buttered-sides up. Press down firmly to compress.

Place a large griddle or frying pan (skillet) over a medium heat. Nestle the sandwiches in the pan and cook for 3–4 minutes, pressing down with a spatula until the bread is golden brown underneath. Carefully flip them over, keeping the sandwich layers together (you may find employing a second spatula or palette knife useful). Gently fry for a further 3 minutes or so, or until the toasties are crisp and golden with molten cheese showing at the edges. Turn down the heat and cook for longer if the cheese hasn't heated through thoroughly enough to melt. Turn off the heat and allow the toasties to rest in the pan for a minute to encourage more melting.

Cut the sandwiches in half then serve straight away with extra rocket on the side.

HERB MAYO HLT

HLT means halloumi, lettuce and tomato. A generously filled, soft sandwich of the Herb Mayonnaise, fresh basil, griddled paprika-halloumi slices, blistered cherry tomatoes and crunchy green lettuce. As you can see, it's a delightful jumble of a sandwich and well worth making. If you can, make a variation of the Herb Mayonnaise using basil and lemon zest. Otherwise, stir finely grated lemon zest, shredded basil and perhaps a little crushed garlic into any bought or homemade mayonnaise.

Serves 2
Preparation time: 20 minutes
Cooking time: 10 minutes

2 tbsp olive oil
1 red chilli, finely chopped
1 garlic clove, crushed
200g (7oz) cherry tomatoes
a small handful of basil leaves, half finely chopped, half shredded
4 large slices of wholemeal sourdough bread
250g (9oz) halloumi, drained and sliced 1cm (½in) thick
1 tsp hot smoked paprika
3–4 tbsp Herb Mayonnaise (page 180)
6 sweet cos lettuce leaves, thickly shredded
sea salt and freshly ground black pepper
Charred Pickles (page 177), drained, to serve

Put 1 tablespoon of the olive oil in a frying pan (skillet) set over a medium heat and add the chilli, garlic and cherry tomatoes. Season with salt and pepper and cook for a minute to soften. Turn up the heat a notch and continue to cook for about 4 minutes until the tomatoes begin to catch and burst. Remove from the heat and add the finely chopped basil, crushing a couple of the tomatoes with the back of a spoon. Tip the mixture into a bowl.

Toast the bread slices under a medium grill or in a toaster until done to your liking on both sides.

Wipe out the frying pan (or use a griddle pan instead) and set over a high heat. Combine the halloumi with the paprika, the remaining tablespoon of olive oil and a generous twist of black pepper. Add to the pan and cook for 1–2 minutes on each side until well browned. Remove from the heat.

Build the sandwich by spreading the toasted bread slices thickly with the mayonnaise. Building on 2 of the slices, start with a lettuce layer, followed by hot halloumi, then tomato confit, the remaining shredded basil and the remaining toast, mayonnaise-side down. Accompany with charred pickled vegetables for crunch and contrast. Messy but good.

TROPICAL OVERNIGHT OATS

These bright and wholesome oats are special enough for a brunch or weekend breakfast. However, you may wish to make a full or half recipe of the oat base to eat over a few days, keeping it chilled. In that case, add grated apple to portions of the base as you go, topping with freshly chopped tropical fruit of your liking, along with dates, toasted coconut and seeds.

Serves 6 generously
Preparation time: 20 minutes
Chilling time: minimum 3 hours
or up to 4 days
Vegan

For the base
300g (10½oz/3 cups) jumbo rolled oats
3 tbsp chia seeds
300ml (10fl oz/1¼ cups) unsweetened
    coconut milk or coconut milk drink
900ml (32fl oz/3¾ cups) pineapple
    juice
a pinch of salt

For the toppings
50g (1¾oz/heaped ⅓ cup) mixed
    seeds, such as sunflower, pumpkin,
    flaxseed (linseed), sesame
30g (1oz/½ cup) coconut flakes
2 large eating (dessert) apples
2 tbsp lemon juice
1 small papaya, seeded and diced
1 small mango, pitted and diced
3 golden kiwi fruit, peeled and sliced
2 large, ripe passion fruit, halved and
    flesh scooped out
3 sticky dates, pitted and torn
    into strips

Combine all the base ingredients, cover and chill overnight or for a minimum of 3 hours or up to 4 days. Stir well before continuing, as the mixture will separate on sitting.

To toast the seeds and coconut flakes for the topping, preheat the oven to 160°C fan (180°C/350°F/gas 4). Spread the seeds out on baking sheet and roast for 2 minutes. Scatter with the coconut flakes and return to the oven for 4 minutes until turning golden. Left to cool, the toasted mixture will keep in an airtight container for a few days.

When you want to eat, prepare the remaining topping ingredients. Coarsely grate the apples, leaving the cores and stalks behind, and toss with the lemon juice. Fold through the oat mixture, then divide between bowls and top with the tropical fruit, torn dates, toasted coconut and seeds.

TOASTED HAZELNUT PORRIDGE
WITH ROAST RHUBARB & STRAWBERRIES

Roast hazelnuts, toasted grains, vanilla, cinnamon and a zinger of a compôte, this makes a cosy weekend breakfast to soothe any nips in the air. You could make the porridge with jumbo rolled oats only, but topping up a third or a half of the base mixture with other rolled grains and grasses – such as rye, quinoa and spelt flakes – adds character and varies your intake of plants.

Serves 4
Preparation time: 15 minutes
Cooking time: 1 hour
Vegan if maple syrup and plant milk used

225g (8oz) strawberries, hulled and halved
6 tbsp maple syrup or mild-flavoured honey
1 vanilla pod (bean), split open and seeds scraped out
200g (7oz) rhubarb, cut into 4cm (2½in) pieces
120g (4oz/scant 1 cup) whole hazelnuts, blanched if liked
180g (6¼oz) mixed porridge grains (see intro)
1.2 litres (40fl oz/4¾ cups) whole milk or unsweetened plant milk
½ tsp ground cinnamon
a pinch of salt

Preheat the oven to 170°C fan (190°C/375°F/gas 5).

In a large ceramic baking dish, toss the strawberries with the maple syrup or honey, the empty vanilla pod and half the scraped out vanilla seeds. Bake uncovered for 15 minutes. Add the rhubarb to the dish with 1 tablespoon of water, combining well, then return the dish to the oven for 25 minutes, stirring gently halfway through. The rhubarb and strawberries should be soft and juicy but not collapsing. Remove the vanilla pod, rinse and set aside.

Meanwhile, spread the hazelnuts out on a baking sheet and roast at the top of the oven for 10 minutes or so until golden and well toasted. Leave to cool, then finely chop one-third of the nuts. Roughly chop the remaining nuts and set these aside.

Spread the mixed porridge grains out on a second baking sheet. Toast for about 10 minutes, stirring halfway through, until pale golden and fragrant.

In a large saucepan, combine the toasted grains with the remaining vanilla seeds and the empty pod, the milk, finely chopped hazelnuts, cinnamon and salt. Bring up to simmering point, stirring. Turn the heat to low, then continue to simmer and stir for about 6 minutes until the porridge is thickened and the grains cooked to your liking. Fish out the vanilla pod if you see it and let the mixture down with a little more hot milk if you prefer a looser texture. Serve the porridge in warm bowls with the fruit compôte and the remaining roughly chopped hazelnuts.

RICOTTA HOTCAKES WITH
SPICED HONEY & RASPBERRIES

Delicate ricotta hotcakes, doused in a buttery ginger, cinnamon and orange-scented honey with plentiful raspberries. This take on a classic is heavily inspired by Bill Granger's famous hotcakes with banana. If possible, have your hotcake fans sitting at the table while you cook, ready to eat when the cakes are still at their puffiest.

Serves 4 (makes 12 hotcakes)
Preparation time: 30 minutes
Cooking time: 20 minutes

For the spiced honey
150g (5oz) orange blossom honey
½ cinnamon stick
2 wide strips of zest and the juice of
    1 orange
10g (½oz) ginger root, peeled and
    finely sliced into discs
70g (2¼oz) salted butter, diced
250g (9oz) raspberries, fresh or frozen

For the pancakes
250g (9oz) ricotta, well drained
3 large eggs, separated
120ml (4fl oz/½ cup) milk
115g (3¾oz/scant 1 cup) plain
    (all-purpose) or spelt flour
¾ tsp baking powder
¼ tsp fine salt
Greek yogurt or crème fraîche,
    to serve

Put the honey in small pan with the cinnamon stick, orange zest and ginger. Bring to the boil over a medium heat and simmer gently for 1 minute. Turn off the heat, cover and leave for 15 minutes (or a good few hours if you have the time). Strain and return to the pan.

To make the pancakes, lightly combine the ricotta with the egg yolks and milk in a large mixing bowl. Don't worry about ricotta lumps. Sift the flour, baking powder and salt over the top.

In a separate bowl, whisk the egg whites until they form stiff peaks. Gently fold half into the ricotta mixture using a large metal spoon or a spatula, retaining as much air as possible. Repeat with the remaining egg white, making an airy, thick batter.

Add 40g (1½oz) of the butter and the orange juice to the honey pan and put it back over a low heat, whisking gently as the butter melts. Simmer gently for 5 minutes, then add 50g (1¾oz) of raspberries and remove from the heat.

To cook the pancakes, use two large frying pans (skillets) if you have them. Otherwise, make batches in one pan. Turn the oven to its lowest setting to keep the first hotcakes warm while you continue frying.

Drop a heaped teaspoon of butter into a frying pan set over a low–medium heat – it should sizzle gently. Tilt the pan so the butter runs across it. Drop 2–3 tablespoons of batter onto the surface to form each hotcake and repeat twice more to make 3 per pan, spacing them out well. Cook the hotcakes for 2½–3 minutes, then deftly flip with a spatula and cook the other side for a further 1–2 minutes. They should be pale-golden and puffed up. If not, adjust the heat accordingly. Ideally, you'd serve these straight from the pan. Otherwise, transfer to a plate, cover loosely with kitchen foil and keep them warm in the oven while you repeat the cooking process until all the hotcakes are done.

Stack up triplets of pancakes on warm plates and douse with the honey mixture, scattering with the remaining raspberries and accompanying with Greek yogurt or crème fraîche, as you like.

GREENS & CHILLI FRITTATA

A frittata is a staple, of course, but for modern tastes, fill the pan to the brim with sweet green vegetables before adding the egg and make the flavours pop with an airy topping of grated Manchego cheese, lemon zest, herb mayonnaise, sprigs of freshness, chilli and shreds of spring onion. It is these finishing touches and fresh textures that make a stylish and elegant version of a breakfast stalwart. You'll need a deep but mini frying pan of 15cm diameter to make the recipe as written. It's one frittata per two portions. Double it to cook in a large (23cm (9in) diameter) pan for four people, but you'll need to bake the frittata in a moderate oven set at 160°C fan (180°C/350°F/gas 4) to get it to set all the way through.

Serves 2
Preparation time: 20 minutes
Cooking time: 10 minutes per frittata

4 spring onions (scallions), trimmed
2 green chillies, 1 finely sliced,
    1 shredded into matchsticks
1 medium courgette (zucchini),
    trimmed
4 large eggs
60g (2oz) Manchego, finely grated
2 tbsp extra virgin olive oil, plus extra
    to serve
1 tsp butter
150g (5oz) podded peas, defrosted
    or fresh
1 garlic clove, finely chopped
a handful of pea shoots
2 tsp finely grated lemon zest and
    2 lemon wedges
a small handful of micro or young
    herbs, such as coriander (cilantro)
    or parsley
1 tbsp Herb Mayonnaise (page 180)
    or Greek yogurt combined with
    chopped herbs
sea salt and freshly ground
    black pepper

Finely slice the white and pale green parts of the spring onions on the diagonal. Slice the remaining green parts into shreds, combine with the chilli shreds and set aside in the fridge. Using a vegetable peeler, pare the courgette into ribbons, not too delicate, if possible, or they will turn mushy.

Beat together the eggs and half the Manchego lightly in a bowl, seasoning well with salt and pepper. Put 1½ tablespoons of olive oil and the butter in a 15cm (6in) diameter, heavy-based frying pan (skillet) set over a high heat. Once foaming, add the courgette and sliced spring onions, stir-frying for a couple of minutes or so until the vegetables begin to catch and soften. Stir in the peas, garlic, sliced chilli and half the pea shoots, frying for a couple of minutes to soften down further.

Turn the heat down to low and slowly pour in the egg mixture, shuffling the pan so that everything finds its level. Cook gently for 3–4 minutes until golden underneath and setting all around the outside. Slide it onto a plate, then place the pan over the frittata and flip it back into the pan. Return to the heat and cook for a further 3–4 minutes until the egg is set and golden underneath. Allow to rest for a couple of minutes.

Combine the remaining Manchego with the lemon zest, spring onion tops and shredded chilli, micro herbs or young herbs and remaining pea shoots. Add a spoonful of herb mayonnaise to the frittata, then sit the green mixture lightly on top like a garden hat. Serve with the lemon wedges and a little extra virgin olive oil, if liked.

MISO & CHARRED GREENS BOWLS

Clichéd it may be – and doesn't that qualify a classic recipe? – but a wholesome café bowl of greens, sesame, avocado and tempeh is a vegan stalwart. You'll need to make the Tahini-Miso Sauce, which literally takes two minutes. I've used fermented soy bean tempeh here, but you could sub in any firm tofu. You can take the girl out of Brighton …

Serves 2 with dressing to spare for other salads
Preparation time: 20 minutes
Cooking time: 10 minutes
Vegan

For the dressing
4 tbsp lemon juice
1½ tbsp sesame oil
1 tbsp groundnut (peanut) oil
1½ tbsp white miso
1 tbsp light soy sauce or tamari
1 tsp maple syrup
1 tsp finely grated ginger root

For the bowls
200g (7oz) tempeh, cut into bite-sized
    pieces
1 tbsp light soy sauce
½ tsp ground turmeric
½ tsp five-spice powder
2 tsp sesame seeds
2 tbsp toasted sesame oil
2 tsp finely chopped ginger root
1 large garlic clove, crushed
1 large head of baby leaf greens, base
    trimmed, leaves thickly shredded
250g (9oz/1¾ cups) steamed
    brown rice
1 ripe avocado, halved, stoned and
    peeled
2 heaped tbsp Tahini-Miso Sauce
    (page 182)
2 spring onions (scallions), trimmed,
    halved and sliced into shreds

To make the dressing, whisk all the dressing ingredients together in a bowl. Taste and see if you like the balance. I have made it punchy and sour, so add a dash more maple syrup to balance, if preferred.

Combine the tempeh pieces with the soy sauce, turmeric and the five-spice. Set aside for 10 minutes, stirring now and then.

To toast the sesame seeds (and I usually toast extra here to have on hand over the next few days), put them in a dry frying pan (skillet) and set over a medium heat. Watch them like a hawk, shaking the pan as they turn oily then begin to colour. In 1–2 minutes they will be golden. Tip onto a plate and set aside.

Return the empty pan to the medium heat with 1 tablespoon of the sesame oil. Add the tempeh and cook for a few minutes until pale golden on all sides. Add half the ginger and half the garlic to the pan, stir-frying for 1–2 minutes to cook out. Tip onto a plate and keep warm. Now wipe out the pan and return it to a high heat, adding the remaining tablespoon of sesame oil. Add the baby greens with the remaining ginger and garlic. You want to fry the leaves so hard they begin to frazzle and char at the edges. Keep them moving constantly. Once slightly wilted (about 3 minutes), remove from the heat. To build each bowl, divide the warm rice and greens between them, adding the tempeh, an avocado half and a spoonful of tahini-miso sauce. Douse with the dressing to taste, scatter with a teaspoon of toasted sesame seeds per bowl and top with shredded spring onions.

BUCKWHEAT & BEETROOT GALETTE

A folded-in crêpe is a vegetarian staple, perhaps with mushrooms, spinach and Gruyère, with or without an egg. This light beetroot and goats' curd variation, spiked with sauerkraut, smoked nuts and Dukkah is a leap but makes for an original brunch. The naturally gluten-free buckwheat galette batter is versatile enough to use wherever you need a reliable crêpe, so keep it on hand for pancake day in savoury or sweet form.

Serves 4
Preparation time: 25 minutes
Cooking time: 1 hour

4 medium beetroot (beets),
    any colour
1 large egg
260ml (9¼fl oz/generous 1 cup)
    whole milk
90g (3¼oz/heaped ⅔ cup) buckwheat
    flour
a pinch of sea salt
a knob of butter
4 tbsp Beetroot Sauerkraut (page 181)
    or ready-made sauerkraut, drained
100g (3½oz) goats' curd or sour cream
a small handful of young chard,
    beetroot (beet) or spinach leaves
a drizzle of extra virgin olive oil
4 tsp Dukkah (page 183) or
    ready-made
50g (1¾oz/⅓ cup) smoked almonds,
    chopped
a small handful of dill fronds,
    chopped

Preheat the oven to 180°C fan (200°C/400°F/gas 6).

Scrub the trimmed beets to remove any dirt but leave the water clinging to them. Wrap three of the wet beetroots in squares of kitchen foil, enclosing each one completely. Set the fourth beetroot aside. Place the parcels on a baking sheet and roast for about 50–60 minutes until tender when a skewer is inserted into the middle. Timings will depend on their size. Leave until cool enough to handle, then peel with a sharp knife, if you like, and cut into dice.

In a mixing bowl, whisk the egg and milk into the flour and salt. Set aside for 30 minutes or cover the batter and put it in the fridge for up to 48 hours, stirring well before use.

To cook each crêpe, place a large frying pan (skillet) over a medium heat. Use a piece of paper towel to wipe about half a teaspoon of butter across the surface of the pan – it should sizzle. Using a small ladle, add just enough batter to cover the pan, swirling to cover the surface in a thin layer (quickly pour any liquid excess back from the pan into the batter bowl if you don't get it quite right at first). Cook the crêpe for a minute or so until set on the surface and turning golden underneath. Loosen at the edges with a palette knife, flip over and cook for another 1–2 minutes until golden. Slide onto a plate lined with paper towels. Repeat another 3 times.

Peel the reserved beetroot and shave into fine slices. Top each galette with beetroots – both roasted and raw – sauerkraut and spoonfuls of goats' curd or sour cream. Tuck in a few salad leaves, drizzling with extra virgin olive oil. Combine the dukkah with the smoked almonds and dill and scatter over the top to serve.

GREEN LENTIL & PEA DHAL

Green lentils make a beautiful dhal, breaking down pleasingly, especially when helped along by a blender to partially blitz the mixture, adding creaminess without the need for any dairy. For me, this is definitely breakfast or brunch food. You might disagree, of course, and prefer to make this for supper. Use any masala or curry powder you love here; the most important thing is to not stint on the sprightly fried curry leaf and runner bean topping – it transforms and brightens this dish.

Serves 4
Preparation time: 20 minutes
Cooking time: 1 hour 30 minutes
Vegan if soy yogurt used

For the dhal
200g (7oz/heaped ¾ cup) dried green
    lentils
3 shallots, halved and finely sliced
3 tbsp groundnut (peanut) oil
1 green chilli, finely chopped
2 tsp finely grated ginger root
3 garlic cloves, crushed
2 tsp finely grated fresh turmeric or
    ½ tsp ground turmeric
2 tsp ground coriander
2 tsp ground cumin
1 tsp brown mustard seeds
2 tsp chaat masala
300g (10½oz) podded peas, fresh
    or frozen
200ml (7fl oz/scant 1 cup) coconut
    milk
2 tbsp lemon juice
2 tbsp finely chopped coriander
    (cilantro) leaves
sea salt and freshly ground
    black pepper

To finish
4 runner beans, trimmed and finely
    sliced diagonally
2 shallots, halved and finely sliced
1 tsp nigella seeds
a small thumb of ginger root, peeled
    and finely shredded
1 green chilli, sliced
½ tsp brown mustard seeds
a handful of fresh curry leaves
a handful of pea shoots
4 tbsp soy or natural yogurt
4 tsp mango chutney
poppadums or warmed roti or naan,
    to serve

To make the dhal, soak the lentils in plenty of cool water for 20 minutes, then rinse and drain well.

Meanwhile, sauté the shallots and a pinch of salt in 2 tablespoons of the oil in a large saucepan set over a low–medium heat. After about 8 minutes they should be soft and sweet but not coloured. Add the green chilli, ginger, garlic and turmeric. Turn the heat up a notch and cook, stirring, for a minute or so. Add the remaining spices and cook for a minute more. Stir in the drained lentils and 900ml (32fl oz/ 3¾ cups) of water. Bring to the boil, then cover, reduce the heat and simmer for 45 minutes, or until the lentils are completely soft.

Stir in the peas and coconut milk and cook for a further 5 minutes. Remove the pan from the heat and, using a hand-held blender, roughly blend about a quarter of the dhal to add a creamy texture. Season with lemon juice, chopped coriander and plenty of salt and pepper to make the flavours sing.

Meanwhile, heat the remaining tablespoon of oil in a large frying pan (skillet) set over a high heat. Add the finishing selection of runner beans, shallots, nigella seeds, ginger and green chilli, stir-frying aggressively for about 3 minutes until sizzling. Add the mustard seeds and curry leaves and cook for 1–2 minutes more until the seeds begin to splutter and pop and the ginger looks frazzled. Season with salt and pepper.

Divide the dhal between warmed bowls and top with the runner bean mixture, pea shoots, spoonfuls of yogurt and mango chutney. Accompany with poppadums or warmed roti or naan bread if you feel those to be more brunch-friendly.

AGRODOLCE PEPPERS
WITH CAPERS & SOURDOUGH

Roast peppers with capers, basil and garlicky croûtons, crisp-edged and soaking up the sweet-sour – *agrodolce* in Italian – dressing. A fried egg makes this breakfast, brunch or lunch, but you could just as well add rocket leaves instead to make a warm salad. I've suggested you use the dairy-free Basil & Lemon Pistou to accompany the plates but any fresh herb pesto, homemade or not, will do.

Serves 4
Preparation time: 20 minutes
Cooking time: 15 minutes
Dairy-free unless standard pesto used

2 massive or 4 normal red (bell)
    peppers, left whole
5 tbsp extra virgin olive oil, plus extra
    to serve
120g (4oz) stale sourdough bread, torn
    into bite-sized pieces
3 garlic cloves, 1 crushed and 2 sliced
1 tbsp capers, rinsed and drained
a large handful of basil leaves
    (or flat-leaf parsley)
2–3 tbsp sherry or red wine vinegar
4 very fresh eggs
1 tbsp mild olive oil
4 tbsp Basil & Lemon Pistou (page 180)
    or ready-made fresh pesto
sea salt and freshly ground
    black pepper

Preheat the oven to 200°C fan (220°C/425°F/gas 7).

Coat the peppers with ½ tablespoon of the olive oil and roast on a baking sheet for 25 minutes or so, flipping halfway through, until the pepper skins are charred and the flesh just beginning to collapse. You don't want them overly soft, as they'll get another stint in a frying pan (skillet). Tip the peppers into a bowl, cover with a plate and set aside to steam for 15 minutes. Remove the cores and seeds and peel away the skins. Cut the flesh into thick pieces.

Turn the oven down to 170°C fan (190°C/375°F/gas 5). Toss the torn bread with 2 tablespoons of olive oil, season with salt and pepper and roast for 6–8 minutes on a baking sheet, stirring halfway through so everything browns evenly. Mix the crushed garlic with an extra ½ tablespoon of oil, then stir it through the mixture and roast for 4–5 minutes more. The bread should be golden and crisp by this time.

Put the sliced garlic, the capers and 2 tablespoons of oil in a large, cold frying pan and set over a low heat. Once the garlic begins to fizz, keep an eye on it. Cook, stirring often, until just beginning to colour and crisp, then turn up the heat and add the roast peppers, most of the basil and 2 tablespoons of the sherry vinegar. Cook down for 1–2 minutes until syrupy, then turn off the heat and leave there.

In a second frying pan set over a medium heat, fry the eggs in the mild olive oil for about 4 minutes until crisp-edged with set whites. Drain on paper towels. Stir the bread into the peppers to coat in the juices thoroughly, then divide among warmed plates, tasting and adding a dash more vinegar, if liked. Add a fried egg to each plate, nestle spoonfuls of pistou or pesto alongside and scatter with extra basil leaves. Finish with a drizzle of extra virgin olive oil, if liked.

LENTIL & SPINACH SHAKSHUKA

Spinach, sweet peppers and tender black lentils are simmered into a spiced tomato base, adding substance to this shakshuka. You can use a pouch of ready-to-eat lentils for ease instead of cooking them from scratch or using tinned. Puy or Beluga are ideal choices as they're small and toothsome. As is customary, the eggs – as fresh as you can find so they hold together – are poached directly into the sauce, but the lentil base would stand alone as a vegan stew to eat with rice. Finish the shakshuka with multiple flourishes to bring it to life: an extra dusting of smoky spice mix, Greek yogurt or labneh, crumbled feta, chopped parsley, chilli flakes, the Fragrant Chilli Oil or Piri Piri Everything sauce.

Serves 4
Preparation time: 10 minutes
Cooking time: 30 minutes

2 tsp cumin seeds
2 tsp coriander seeds
¾ tsp ground cinnamon
2 tsp smoked paprika
2–3 tbsp olive oil
1 red onion, halved and finely sliced
1–2 red chillies, finely chopped
2 red romano peppers, finely sliced
4 garlic cloves, finely chopped
1 tsp dried chilli (hot pepper) flakes
    (chipotle if possible)
a small bunch of flat-leaf parsley,
    stalks finely sliced, leaves
    roughly chopped
2 × 400g (14oz) tins of chopped
    tomatoes
250g (9oz/1¼ cups) cooked and
    drained Puy or Beluga lentils
150g (5oz) baby leaf spinach
4 very fresh eggs
3 tbsp strained Greek yogurt or labneh
150g (5oz) feta, crumbled
3 tbsp Fragrant Chilli Oil (page 172)
    or ready-made OR 3 tbsp Piri
    Piri Everything (page 176) or any
    mildish hot sauce, homemade or
    ready-made
sea salt and freshly ground
    black pepper
griddled flatbreads, to serve

Start by making a spice mix. Toast the cumin seeds, coriander seeds, ground cinnamon and smoked paprika in a dry frying pan (skillet) for 1 minute or so until fragrant. Grind in a pestle and mortar.

Put 2–3 tablespoons of olive oil in a large frying pan with a lid (about 25cm (10in) in diameter) and set over a low–medium heat. Add the onion, chilli and peppers with a pinch of salt and cook, stirring often, for 10–15 minutes until very soft but not browned.

Add half the toasted spice mix, the garlic, ½ teaspoon of chilli flakes and the finely chopped parsley stalks and cook for a few minutes, stirring. Add the tomatoes, season with salt and pepper, turn the heat up a notch and simmer for about 7 minutes until the tomato mixture has begun to thicken. Tip in the lentils and spinach and simmer for a couple more minutes, stirring to wilt the leaves evenly.

To poach the eggs, you'll need to work one hollow and one egg at a time as the indents will 'refill' with sauce quickly and cloud the egg whites. Crack an egg into a ladle and use the base of the ladle to make a deep crater in the sauce. Immediately slip the egg from the ladle into the space. You'll need to make four hollows in total so space each one out accordingly. Cover the pan with a lid, reduce the heat to low and cook for 6–7 minutes, or until the whites are firm throughout and the yolks are set to your liking. Remove the lid, scatter the shakshuka with the roughly chopped parsley leaves, spoonfuls of yogurt or labneh, a scattering of the remaining spice mix, crumbled feta and the remaining chilli flakes. If you have it, add spoonfuls of fragrant chilli oil or Piri Piri Everything or any mildish hot sauce. Go as wild as you like. Serve with griddled flatbreads for scooping.

SMALL PLATES

A stunning but rather motley collection of small plates and bowlfuls, comprising starters, snacks, soups, dips and other delectable, crisp delights. This is where you'll find lacy-edged fritters and patties, spring rolls, falafels, alluring alternatives to hummus, tacos, salads and some cracking soups. Kaleidoscopic they may be as a collective, but every single one has a place in your repertoire.

Let's start with the fritter and falafel contingent. Deep-frying, or even shallow-frying, at home isn't something I undertake lightly. Treating oneself to fried food now and then isn't so much the issue, especially when it involves a vegetable fritter to be eaten with salad, rather than a fast-food doughnut. It's the chip shop smell and the faff of cooling then filtering oil I resent more than any other kitchen task. If I have stipulated frying in a recipe – and they tend to be concentrated in this chapter. Know that either the results are more than worth it or it is essential to the success of the recipe. Or both. I wouldn't ask you to do it otherwise.

Instead of serving them as starters or light lunches, you may prefer to combine some of these recipes to make a more expansive meal, as I have suggested in Chapter 4, Sides. A stylish Bitter Leaf Salad with Pear, Grape, Blue Cheese & Honeyed Walnuts is just made for a carefully selected cheeseboard, instead of chutneys and fresh fruit. A raw Shaved Cauliflower Salad with Dates works as a starter, side or lunch by itself, but try it with the Beetroot, Walnut & Harissa Dip as the weather cools. Tomato Fritters with Feta & Olives make a natural partner for, or precursor to, a delectable Greek Rusk Salad. You'll need to be a feta fan to enjoy this idea, but you could swap one of those out for the Split Pea Purée with Caramelised Shallots & Capers for less in the way of salted cheese.

I'm especially proud of the four soups featured here. They are all magnificent and deserve to be made. The Hearty Bean Soup will warm you through for the whole day and gets better and better as it sits. The other three soups – Baked Shallot Soup with Tarragon Toasts, Roast Pumpkin & Pepper Soup with Gruyère Toasts and Smoky Seeds and Roast Cauliflower, Onion & Chickpea Soup – will all take you from lunch to dinner party. Though they are all distinct and entirely different, there is a similar technique underpinning all of them and it's so successful I couldn't resist using it on repeat: use your oven to roast vegetables for vegetarian soup bases instead of softening them on a stovetop. The process of roasting caramelises naturally sweet vegetables, such as winter squash, alliums and cauliflower, so thoroughly and profoundly, I promise you'll never use another technique for an autumnal or winter soup.

GREEK RUSK SALAD

I'm not sure when a Greek-style salad with the rusk included was overlooked in favour of its much-imitated, ruskless cousin, but I don't think it was the right choice. Once tossed with an olive oil dressing, the rusks turn soft on the outside, toothsome on the inside, and are utterly perfect with the ripest tomatoes and feta. I favour the wholegrain barley rusks here. They aren't too tricky to find – any Greek deli or online store will have them – and because they are dried, any extra will keep extremely well for the next salad. Alternatively, spread with sundried tomato paste, olive oil, a touch of vinegar and dried oregano, leaving the rusks to soften and soak, before topping with crumbled feta for breakfast.

Serves 4 generously, or 8 as part of a salad-y lunch
Preparation time: 20 minutes
Macerating time: at least 30 minutes or up to 2 hours

150ml (5fl oz/scant ⅔ cup) extra virgin olive oil, plus extra to serve
5 tbsp red wine vinegar
120g (4oz) rusks, broken into large, bite-sized chunks
3 tbsp best-quality sundried tomato purée (paste)
2 tsp dried oregano
400g (14oz) ripest tomatoes, sliced into wedges, according to size
1 midi cucumber, quartered and thickly sliced
a large handful of Kalamata olives, drained
2 tbsp capers, rinsed and drained
400g (14oz) best-quality feta cheese, drained and cut into 4 slabs
sea salt and freshly ground black pepper

Start by making the dressing. Combine the olive oil with the vinegar, seasoning with salt and pepper.

Put the rusk in a large bowl and toss with half the dressing mixture, the tomato purée and 1 teaspoon of dried oregano. Set aside for at least 30 minutes to soften, tossing every now and then to coat evenly. Ideally, you'd leave it longer – for up to a couple of hours – so that the rusk softens properly in places, staying crisp in others. Taste every now and then to check it's to your liking.

To create the salad, add the tomatoes, cucumber, olives and capers to the bowl with the rusk, tossing through gently to combine. Arrange on a serving platter or divide between serving bowls, topping with the slabs of feta, the remaining oregano and the remaining dressing. Season with pepper and serve with little bowls for the olive stones.

TOMATO FRITTERS WITH FETA & OLIVES

These fragrant, crisp fritters are heavily inspired by the Greek *tomatokeftedes*, enjoyed with a Santorini view. I've added far more herbs than is common and served them on a bed of salted yogurt for contrast. Be generous with those summer herbs in the batter; use basil, parsley, dill, Greek basil, mint or (only a little) oregano or marjoram, in any combination. Two handfuls can also be interpreted as a gently packed 250ml (9fl oz/1 cup) by volume. The grated courgette is not so traditional but adds lightness and texture. I have had success grating in half a firm aubergine (eggplant) in place of it.

Serves 4 (makes about 16 fritters)
Preparation time: 25 minutes
Cooking time: 10 minutes

For the feta yogurt
200g (7oz/scant 1 cup) thick
  Greek yogurt
100g (3½oz) feta, drained and
  crumbled
freshly ground black pepper

For the fritters
200g (7oz) ripest tomatoes, chopped
  into thumbnail-sized pieces
1 small red onion, halved and
  finely sliced
1 garlic clove, crushed
1 pinch of dried chilli (hot pepper)
  flakes
1 medium courgette (zucchini),
  trimmed and coarsely grated
2 handfuls of chopped fresh summer
  herbs, plus a few sprigs to serve
  (see intro)
100–125g (3½–4½oz/scant 1 cup–
  1 cup) self-raising flour
about 150ml (5fl oz/scant ⅔ cup)
  groundnut (peanut) oil, for frying
sea salt and freshly ground
  black pepper
caper berries, rinsed and drained,
  to serve
a drizzle of extra virgin olive oil,
  to finish

To make the yogurt, which can be finished up to 3 days ahead, blitz 2 tablespoons of the yogurt and the feta together until smooth. Fold into the remaining yogurt in a mixing bowl and add a few twists of pepper to season. Cover and keep chilled until needed.

To make the fritters, put the tomatoes in a large mixing bowl and give them a bruising stir so that they give out some tomato juice. Combine with the onion, garlic, chilli flakes, courgette and herbs, adding a generous seasoning of salt and pepper. Leave to sit for a few minutes so that the vegetables give out some of their water. Stir well, then scatter in 100g (3½oz/scant 1 cup) of the flour and lightly mix through with a spatula. A thick, nobbly batter should form. Don't over-mix or the fritters will be dense, but if the mixture appears too wet, gradually add up to 25g (1oz/2 tbsp) more flour.

Put the oil in a heavy-based frying pan (skillet) over a medium heat. It should be about 2cm (¾in) deep and sizzle when a tiny bit of batter is dropped in, then take about 30 seconds to turn golden.

Drop tablespoons of batter into the pan a few at a time, keeping them well separated, and fry until golden brown on both sides. This should take around 3 minutes in total so adjust the heat as needed. When golden and crisp, remove them from the pan using a slotted spoon and drain on a plate lined with paper towels.

Serve the hot fritters on a base of the cool feta yogurt, scattered with caper berries and extra herb sprigs. You can do this as individual servings or one large one. Either way, finish the platter or plates off with a drizzle of extra virgin olive oil.

SPLIT PEA PURÉE WITH CARAMELISED SHALLOTS & CAPERS

Crisp capers and shallots are scattered over this intensely savoury Greek dip. You could add dried oregano at the end, too. Serve with pillows of griddled flatbread for scooping. The yellow split lentils or peas used here are known as 'fava' in Greece – not to be confused with broad beans – hence its more common name as a fava bean purée or dip. I have used caper leaves in the sizzling topping here but only because I had long since bought a tiny jar and thought them beautiful. A few extra capers will more than suffice.

Serves 4
Preparation time: 30 minutes
Cooking time: 1 hour
Vegan

200g (7oz/scant 1 cup) split peas, rinsed under cool running water in a sieve
600ml (20fl oz/2½ cups) vegetable stock
4 large shallots, 2 roughly chopped, 2 finely sliced
3 large garlic cloves, chopped
about 100ml (3½fl oz/scant ½ cup) extra virgin olive oil, plus extra to serve
2 tbsp capers, rinsed and drained
1 tbsp caper leaves if available, rinsed and drained (see intro)
juice of 2 lemons
sea salt and freshly ground black pepper
griddled flatbreads, to serve

Put the split peas in a large saucepan or heatproof bowl, cover generously with just-boiled water and set aside for 20 minutes. Tip the peas into a colander in the sink, rinsing again under the cool tap and draining well.

Transfer the peas to a large saucepan and add the vegetable stock, roughly chopped shallots and garlic. Bring to the boil over a low–medium heat, then skim off and discard any foam from the top using a large spoon. Now cover the pan, turn the heat down a little and simmer gently for about 50 minutes, or until the peas are completely soft and breaking down. If they are older, they may take a little longer to cook, but I have tried to account for a good range of ages in this cooking time.

Meanwhile, put about 2 tablespoons of olive oil in a large frying pan (skillet) and add the sliced shallots with a large pinch of salt. Place over a medium heat and cook, stirring often, until the shallots are beginning to frazzle and turn golden. This should take around 10 minutes. Turn up the heat and add the capers with the caper leaves if you have them. It matters not a jot if you don't. Fry briskly for 1–2 minutes until the contents of the pan crisp up a little more. Set aside in the pan.

Remove the cooked peas from the heat and leave to stand for 10 minutes. Add 70ml (2¼fl oz/scant ⅓ cup) of the olive oil, the lemon juice and a good seasoning of salt and pepper. Either go in with a hand-held blender or blend in an upright blender. If you have a high-speed version of the latter, it will produce the best consistency so it's worth the faff. Taste for seasoning and adjust as needed (it can take quite a lot of salt). Cover the surface of the soupy purée with an upturned plate to prevent a skin forming, then set aside to cool for 3 hours. It will thicken right up to a dipping (hummus) consistency and will thicken even further if chilled. The chilled purée will keep for a few days, but make sure it's at room temperature to serve.

When ready to use, stir the dip well. Transfer to serving dishes or plates. Put the shallot pan back on the heat until the contents just start to sizzle again. Spoon over the dip with a generous drizzle of olive oil. Offer griddled flatbreads alongside for scooping as a snack, side or as part of a mezze selection.

GREEN RED LENTIL FALAFEL

Though herb-flecked and spiked with toasted pumpkin seeds, hence the green description, these crunchy falafels have a similar texture to those made 'properly' with soaked dried chickpeas (garbanzos), but are based on the ubiquitous red lentil. They are superb but I can't guarantee they would work if oven baked. To put it another way, I wouldn't encourage frying if it wasn't worth it and essential.

Offset their delicious crunch with a selection of soft flatbreads, unconventional chimichurri (it works), cool, creamy yogurt and a swoosh of pumpkin seed dukkah, amended from The Sauce. Feel free to tinker with a bought dukkah, crushing the toasted pumpkin seeds into it.

Makes 20, serving 6 as a starter, or 4 as a main with other mezze
Preparation time: 30 minutes, plus 2 hours soaking
Cooking time: 25 minutes
Vegan without yogurt or labneh

250g (9oz/1 cup) red lentils
50g (1¾oz/⅓ cup) pumpkin seeds
2 tsp cumin seeds
2 tsp coriander seeds
4 tbsp chickpea (gram) flour
1 small white onion, finely chopped
3 garlic cloves, crushed
1 mild green chilli, chopped
1 tsp bicarbonate of soda (baking soda)
1 tsp salt
a handful of coriander (cilantro) leaves, chopped
a handful of flat-leaf parsley leaves, chopped
sea salt and freshly ground black pepper

To serve
2 large flatbreads, charred on a griddle
2 heaped tbsp Chimichurri (page 169) or ready-made
2 heaped tbsp labneh or strained Greek yogurt
a handful of fresh herbs, such as flat-leaf parsley or thyme leaves
2 tbsp Dukkah (page 183) or ready-made
2 tbsp pumpkin seeds, toasted and chopped

Put the lentils in a bowl, cover generously with cold water and set aside to soak for 2 hours. Rinse in a sieve under cool running water and drain thoroughly.

Put the pumpkin, cumin and coriander seeds in a dry frying pan (skillet) over a medium heat. Toast, shaking the pan often, for 1–2 minutes until fragrant and a shade darker. Tip into a food processor with the drained lentils, chickpea flour, onion, garlic, chilli, bicarbonate of soda, salt, coriander and parsley. Season with black pepper. Pulse, stopping every few pulses to redistribute the mixture around the blades with a spatula, until the mixture is very finely chopped and beginning to clump together. No lentil shapes should remain but you don't want a complete mush. Transfer to a container, cover and chill for an hour, if you have time. This will help the falafel to hold together when frying but isn't essential.

To shape the falafel, I find it easiest to use two tablespoons to firmly form 'quenelle' shapes, rolling the torpedo shape from one spoon to the other until fully formed. You should get around 20.

Turn the oven to its lowest setting and line a large baking sheet with paper towels to drain the falafel on.

Fill a medium-sized, deep, heavy-based saucepan with enough oil to fill it to a 6cm (2½in) depth. Heat the oil to 180°C (350°F) or to the point at which a cube of white bread turns golden in about 30 seconds. Fry the falafel in batches of five, turning them with a slotted spoon, for 4–5 minutes until deeply browned and crisp all over. Use a slotted spoon to carefully transfer to the sheet lined with paper towels and keep warm in the oven while you cook the remainder.

Serve the hot falafel with griddled flatbreads, spoonfuls of chimichurri and labneh or yogurt, extra herbs for garnish and a generous flourish of dukkah combined with the toasted and chopped pumpkin seeds.

ROAST CAULIFLOWER, ONION & CHICKPEA SOUP

A velvet-smooth, creamy vegan soup with crisp chilli kale. The kale is to round off the soup, roasted in the oven and placed in the middle of each bowl. Keep the extra cooled kale crisps in an airtight container to eat later.

Serves 4 (makes about 1.5l
(56fl oz/6⅔ cups)
Preparation time: 30 minutes
Cooking time: 1 hour 30 minutes
Vegan

For the soup
4 tbsp olive oil
3 small brown onions, trimmed and
   halved, with skins left on
550g (1lb 4oz) cauliflower florets and
   stalk (1 small, trimmed head)
1½ tsp coriander seeds
1½ tsp cumin seeds
½ tsp dried chilli (hot pepper) flakes
3 whole garlic cloves, skins on
950ml (32fl oz/4 cups) vegetable stock
450g (1lb/3¼ cups) cooked chickpeas
   (garbanzos), drained (about
   2 × 400g (14oz) tins, drained,
   if using tinned)
a squeeze of lemon juice (1–2 tbsp)
sea salt and freshly ground
   black pepper

For the chilli kale crisp topping
100g (3½oz) kale, trimmed
1 tbsp olive oil
1 tsp dried chilli (hot pepper) flakes
1 tsp smoked paprika
Fragrant Chilli Oil (page 172) or
   ready-made, to serve

Preheat the oven to 170°C fan (190°C/375°F/gas 5).

Put 1½ tablespoons of the olive oil (if you're measuring – a generous glug is fine if you're not into that) at one end of a large roasting tin. Sit the onions on top of the oil, cut-sides down and bunched up together. Cover with a sheet of kitchen foil, tucking in around the edges, and roast for 40 minutes until the onions have begun to soften and turn golden underneath.

Meanwhile, toss the cauliflower florets with another 2 tablespoons of olive oil, the coriander seeds, cumin seeds and chilli flakes in a large bowl, seasoning with salt and pepper.

Remove the foil from the onions and spread the cauliflower mixture out in the roasting tin in a single layer. Return to the oven for 25 minutes.

Add the whole garlic cloves and flip the vegetables over, including the onions. Cook for a final 20 minutes until the vegetables are soft and golden.

Leave until cool enough to peel the onions and the garlic, then transfer everything but these peelings to a large saucepan. Add the stock and chickpeas and bring to the boil over a low heat. Simmer for 10 minutes until the vegetables and chickpeas are totally soft.

Meanwhile, make the chilli kale crisps to top the soup while the oven is hot. Tear the kale into bite-sized pieces, then toss with the olive oil, chilli flakes and paprika. Season with salt and pepper. Spread the kale out in a large roasting tin, making sure it is in a single layer with space between the leaves. Bake for 6–8 minutes, shuffling halfway, until crisp and just beginning to brown. Do note that this time can vary slightly according to how delicate or tough your kale leaves are so keep an eye for the first shuffle after 2 minutes and expect to add a few minutes in total for very tough kale leaves. Set aside to cool in the pan. The kale will continue to crisp up further.

When the soup is ready, using a high-speed, upright blender for the best texture, blitz half the soup at a time, transferring the first batch back to the saucepan once velvety smooth. Repeat with the remaining soup, then gently warm through over a low heat until piping hot. (You can also blend in the pan using a hand-held blender – it just won't be quite as velveteen.) Taste the soup and adjust the seasoning as needed. A squeeze of lemon juice will perk the flavours up.

Serve the soup in warmed bowls, topped with crisp kale and a dash of chilli oil.

BAKED SHALLOT SOUP WITH TARRAGON TOASTS

The idea here, and it's been a successful one, was to imbue the soup with similar umami depth and resonance to a traditional French onion soup recipe. I've employed several tricks to achieve this in vegetarian fashion: slow roasting shallots to tease out their sugars and caramelise them, the sweet and umami hits of sundried tomato paste and miso, a little flour to add body to the stock and a long, slow simmer to make sure the finished texture is melting and tender. Bright goats' curd toasts with the numb hum of tarragon add freshness where traditional melted Gruyère would be too rich.

Serves 4 (makes 1.2 litres/40fl oz/
4¾ cups)
Preparation time: 25 minutes
Cooking time: 1 hour 15 minutes

3 tbsp olive oil
2 rosemary sprigs
10 medium-sized banana shallots
 (echalions), halved
1 tbsp plain (all-purpose) flour
2 tsp white miso paste
1 heaped tsp sundried tomato purée
 (paste)
150ml (5fl oz/scant ⅔ cup) dry white
 wine or dry sherry
850ml (29fl oz/3½ cups) vegetable stock
100g (3½oz) sourdough bread or
 French baguette, sliced into 4
½ garlic clove
100g (3½oz) soft goats' cheese or
 goats' curd
1 tbsp finely chopped tarragon leaves
sea salt and freshly ground
 black pepper

Preheat the oven to 170°C fan (190°C/375°F/gas 5).

Drizzle the base of a large, sturdy roasting tin (preferably one that can stand up to sitting on a hot hob afterwards) with 2 tablespoons of the olive oil. Add the rosemary sprigs and season with salt and pepper. Sit the halved shallots on the oil, cut-sides down. They should be packed quite snugly in a single layer.

Brush or drizzle the tops with a further tablespoon of olive oil, cover tightly with kitchen foil and roast for about 40 minutes until softened and starting to caramelise underneath. Uncover and roast for a further 10 minutes. The top layers of shallot should be coming away. Remove the rosemary sprigs from the pan, add the flour and mash the shallots down roughly with a potato masher or the back of a spoon.

If your pan is sturdy enough, place it directly over a low heat on the hob and stir in the miso paste, sundried tomato purée, wine or sherry and stock. If not, transfer the shallot mixture to a large saucepan before adding the other ingredients over the heat. Bring to the boil, then simmer gently for 20 minutes until slightly thickened. Taste and adjust the seasoning. The soup should be sweet and savoury and the shallots so soft they are melting into it.

Toast or grill the bread slices until well browned. Rub all over with the cut side of the garlic clove half. Combine the goats' cheese or curd with the tarragon, season with black pepper and spread thickly over the toasts. Ladle the soup into warmed bowls and float the toasts on top to serve.

SHAVED CAULIFLOWER SALAD WITH DATES

A stunning and easy raw cauliflower salad, resplendent with sweet dates, spices, toasted barley and preserved lemon, this makes a dazzling summer lunch with other salads and/or mezze, especially when made with purple cauliflower, as in the picture here.

Serves 4
Preparation time: 20 minutes
Cooking time: 25 minutes
Vegan if maple syrup or agave used

200g (7oz/1¼ cups) pearl barley
4 tbsp extra virgin olive oil, plus extra
   to serve
500ml (17fl oz/2 cups) vegetable stock
1½ tsp coriander seeds
½ tsp ground allspice
600g (1lb 5oz) purple or white
   cauliflower (1 large), trimmed and
   quartered
1 garlic clove, crushed
1 red chilli, finely chopped
2 small preserved lemons, drained
   and chopped
1½ tbsp maple syrup, agave or honey
finely grated zest and juice of 1 lemon
a large handful of flat-leaf parsley
   leaves, chopped
5 Medjool dates, pitted and sliced
3 tbsp Dukkah (page 183) or
   ready-made
2 tbsp shelled pistachios, chopped
sea salt and freshly ground
   black pepper

Put the barley in a medium saucepan with 1 tablespoon of the oil and set it over a medium heat. Toast, stirring often to coat the grains in the oil and prevent them catching. The barley should be golden and smelling nutty but not scorched. Add the stock, bring to the boil, cover and simmer for 20–25 minutes. The grains should be tender but not too soft and the liquid should have been absorbed. Set aside to cool slightly.

Put the coriander seeds in a dry frying pan (skillet) and place over a medium heat to toast for 1 minute. Add the ground allspice and toast for around 30 seconds more until the spices are fragrant but not burnt. Remove and crush roughly with the base of a jar or in a pestle and mortar.

Slice the quartered cauliflower as thinly as possible with a sharp knife, using the central core to keep the slices together as much as possible. Some of the cauliflower will inevitably disintegrate into rubble. This is fine and all adds to the texture.

Combine the garlic, chilli, preserved lemon, maple syrup, fresh lemon zest and juice and remaining 3 tablespoons of olive oil in a bowl. Toss the cauliflower, barley, toasted spices, parsley and dressing together. Season with black pepper and taste before adding salt as the preserved lemons add quite a hit. Arrange on a platter, tumbling the dates through right at the end so they don't turn fuzzy. Finish with the dukkah and chopped pistachios.

GREEN TACOS

The contrast of cool, silky avocado and lime, charred vegetables and pickles with the shatter of well-fried tacos is magical, but you can also steam the little tortillas if you prefer. My favourite way to do this is by stacking them all up on a small plate, covering with an upturned bowl and microwaving on high for just under 2 minutes until steaming hot and softened. Check them after a minute as a powerful microwave can cook them in less time.

If you haven't pickled any onions ahead of time (this recipe uses the Pink Pickles), make a cheat's version as I have described elsewhere: slice a halved red onion finely and toss with a fat pinch of sugar (any kind), a fat pinch of salt and a splash of red wine vinegar. Set aside for at least 20 minutes, stirring occasionally, then drain to use in the tacos.

Serves 4 (makes 8 tacos)
Preparation time: 40 minutes
Cooking time: 15 minutes
Vegan

For the avocado cream
2 large, ripe avocados, halved,
    stoned and peeled
1 small garlic clove, crushed
juice of 1 lime
1 green chilli, chopped
a small handful of coriander (cilantro)
    leaves and stalks, chopped

For the courgettes
2 medium courgettes (zucchini),
    trimmed and cut into chunky
    5cm (2in) batons
3 tbsp olive oil
16 padron peppers
1 garlic clove, crushed
2 tsp chopped oregano leaves
a squeeze of lemon or lime juice

For the tortillas
8 × 8cm (3in) diameter corn tortillas
5 tbsp groundnut (peanut) oil
salt and freshly ground black pepper
2–3 tbsp Pink Pickles (page 168),
    drained, to serve
a handful of coriander (cilantro)
    sprigs, to serve

To make the avocado cream, put all the ingredients in a high-speed blender or the small bowl of a food processor and blend until silky-smooth, stopping to scrape down the sides as needed. Season to taste with salt and pepper, then cover and refrigerate for up to 2 hours until needed.

In a bowl, toss the courgettes with 2 tablespoons of the olive oil and a generous amount of salt and pepper. In a separate bowl, coat the padron peppers with the final tablespoon of olive oil. Season with salt and pepper.

Place a frying pan (skillet) over a high heat until smoking hot. Add the courgettes in a single layer (divide into two batches to cook, if needed) and cook for a total of 5–6 minutes, turning every minute or so until highly coloured and tender. Add the garlic and oregano to the pan, tossing to distribute it evenly among the courgettes. Cook for a further 30 seconds or so, then tip the lot into a bowl and keep it warm. Add the peppers to the empty pan and cook for 3 minutes or so, turning halfway, until blackened and softened. Tip into the courgette bowl with a squeeze of lemon or lime juice. Wipe out the frying pan.

To cook the tortillas, put the groundnut oil in the frying pan and return to a medium heat. Have a plate lined with paper towels ready and, once the oil is shimmering, fry the tortillas in two or three batches for about 3 minutes, turning with tongs until they are golden and crisp on both sides. Transfer to the plate to drain thoroughly.

To assemble, lay the crisp tortillas on a serving platter or plate. Top each with a little avocado cream, then pile a couple of padron peppers and a few courgette batons on top. Finish with some pink pickles and coriander sprigs. You might want to serve these 'family style' so everyone can assemble their own.

CORN FRITTERS WITH GOATS' CHEESE & OLIVES

These toasted sweetcorn and polenta fritters can be used as the basis for a brunch or lunch as below, or made as little canapés with the toasted corn and olive salsa spooned on top (similar to blinis). For reference, three corn cobs produce around 350g (12oz) of shaved corn kernels. You can use fresh, defrosted frozen or tinned and well-drained corn, but I'd encourage you to make this when sweetcorn is in season to take advantage of its flavour and value.

Serves 3–4 (makes about 18 fritters)
Preparation time: 30 minutes
Cooking time: 15 minutes

about 120ml (4fl oz/½ cup) neutral oil such as groundnut (peanut) oil, for frying
3 sweetcorn cobs, kernels sliced off
100g (3½oz) black olives, stoned and chopped
6 spring onions (scallions), trimmed and finely sliced
2 tsp chopped oregano leaves
180g (6¼oz) mature goats' cheese log, cut or crumbled into 1cm (½in) pieces
100g (3½oz/½ cup) natural kefir (or thin yogurt)
100g (3½oz/⅔ cup) medium polenta or cornmeal
1½ tbsp chickpea (gram) flour
1½ tbsp cornflour (cornstarch)
a pinch of dried chilli (hot pepper) flakes (optional)
1 tsp baking powder
2 large eggs, separated
juice of 1 lemon
2 tbsp extra virgin olive oil
sea salt and freshly ground black pepper
snipped mustard sprouts, to serve

Put 1 tablespoon of oil in a large frying pan (skillet) over a high heat. Once shimmering, add the sweetcorn kernels and fry for about 5 minutes, stirring now and then, until the kernels turn golden brown all over and begin to pop (stand back from the pan if this happens!). Remove from the heat.

Set aside one-third of the toasted sweetcorn, then add half the olives, half the spring onions, half the oregano and 60g (2oz) of the goats' cheese pieces.

Put the remaining two-thirds of the toasted and cooled sweetcorn kernels and the kefir into a mini food processor or the small bowl of a food processor. A hand-held blender will also work here. Blitz to a very rough purée. Transfer to a mixing bowl with the polenta or cornmeal, chickpea flour, cornflour and chilli flakes, if using. Fold in the baking powder with the remaining spring onions, olives, oregano and goats' cheese, adding two generous pinches of salt and lots of black pepper.

In a separate, large and clean bowl, whisk the egg whites until they hold stiff peaks. Make a well in the middle of the sweetcorn mixture and add the egg yolks, gradually stirring them in, then use a spatula or large metal spoon to fold in the whipped egg whites, preserving as much air as possible, to make a thick batter.

Preheat the oven to its lowest setting to keep the cooked fritters warm and line an ovenproof plate with paper towels.

Add enough neutral oil – this should be around a third of the remainder – to a large frying pan to cover the base and place over a medium–high heat. Spoon heaped tablespoons of about a third of the batter into the pan, spacing them out well to make about 6 fritters. They should sizzle nicely. Fry for 2–3 minutes until golden brown on the base, then flip over and cook for a further 2 minutes or so. Transfer to the prepared plate and keep warm in the oven while you cook the remaining fritters in two further batches.

Add the lemon juice and extra virgin olive oil to the toasted sweetcorn and olive mixture and season to taste with salt and pepper. Serve the hot fritters with this salsa and a delicate pile of snipped mustard sprouts.

GREEN HUMMUS

Apart from needing a turbo-charged, high-speed blender to make the smoothest of dips (this is an unfortunate truth, rather like finding out that a fancy bike does, in fact, make you a better cyclist when people said it was about leg strength all along), the best hummus trick I can give you is to make sure your chickpeas are both warm and completely tender when you blend them. This way they will emulsify with the tahini to form a light and airy texture that cold, hard chickpeas could never attain. Jars of chickpeas tend to be softer than tinned versions and are only a little more costly. To create the crunchiest of radishes for dipping, drop them into a bowl of iced water for 15 minutes or so before draining and eating.

Serves 4 as a snack with crudités
Preparation time: 20 minutes
Cooking time: 10 minutes
Vegan

For the hummus
660g (1lb 6oz) jar of chickpeas
    (garbanzos)
2 tbsp extra virgin olive oil, plus extra
    to serve
1 tsp cumin seeds
100g (3½oz) baby spinach leaves
120g (4oz) tahini
1 garlic clove, crushed
juice of ½ lemon
a handful of parsley, mint or basil
    leaves, chopped
sea salt and freshly ground
    black pepper

To serve
a handful of radishes, trimmed
4 baby cucumbers, halved
2 red chicory (Belgian endive) bulbs,
    trimmed and leaves separated

Scoop the chickpeas and their liquid from the jar into a small saucepan, top up with water, if necessary, to almost cover the chickpeas and bring up to simmering point over a low heat. If the chickpeas aren't very soft already, cover with a lid and simmer for 5–10 minutes until they soften. Otherwise, simply heat through thoroughly. Keep warm.

Put 1 tablespoon of olive oil in a frying pan (skillet) set over a medium heat, add the cumin seeds and fry for 1 minute. Add the spinach leaves with 1 tablespoon of water and stir-fry for a couple of minutes until the leaves are completely wilted.

Drain the chickpeas, reserving 4 tablespoons of the cooking water.

Tip the wilted spinach mixture into a food processor or high-speed blender with the warm chickpeas and their 4 tablespoons of liquid, the remaining olive oil, the tahini, garlic and lemon juice. Season lightly and blend for a few minutes until completely smooth and silky, stopping to scrape down the sides with a spatula now and then so that everything purées evenly. Add the herbs and blend again until they are almost completely smooth. Taste and adjust the seasoning as needed. Allow to cool a little (it will thicken on cooling), then transfer the hummus to a serving bowl.

Drizzle with extra olive oil and serve with the raw vegetables for dipping.

TOFU WITH MISO MUSHROOMS

Golden tofu slabs with an umami-rich wild mushroom and miso broth mixture spooned over. Serve as a starter or elegant lunch, or to eat as a generous main course for two, add steamed rice and greens alongside. Leftovers are excellent the following day if you have future lunches in mind.

Serves 2
Preparation time: 25 minutes
Cooking time: 25 minutes
Vegan

15g (½ oz) dried woodland or porcini
   mushrooms
½ tsp ground turmeric
2 tbsp toasted sesame oil
2 tbsp light soy sauce
400g (14oz) extra-firm tofu, drained
   and cut into 4
1½ tbsp groundnut (peanut) oil or any
   mild oil
2 garlic cloves, sliced
a small thumb of ginger root, peeled
   and finely grated
200g (7oz) mixed wild or woodland
   mushrooms, halved or sliced if large
2 tsp miso paste
2 tbsp mirin
a pinch of sugar (optional)
a few coriander (cilantro) sprigs
2 small handfuls of alfalfa or mustard
   sprouts
sea salt and freshly ground
   black pepper
steamed greens and brown rice,
   to serve (optional)

Crumble the dried mushrooms into a jug and top up with 200ml (7fl oz/scant 1 cup) of just-boiled water from the kettle. Set aside for a minimum of 10 minutes.

Meanwhile, combine the turmeric with 1 tablespoon of the sesame oil and 1 tablespoon of the soy sauce in a wide bowl. Add the tofu and coat in the marinade, setting aside for 30 minutes or even covering and chilling overnight if you have the time.

Preheat the oven to its lowest setting for warming. Place a large frying pan (skillet) over a medium heat, adding half the groundnut oil. Season the tofu with salt and pepper and add to the frying pan – it should sizzle. Keep any marinade liquid left behind. Cook the tofu for 4–5 minutes on each side, flipping carefully with a spatula, until golden and crisp. Remove to a plate and keep warm in the low oven. Wipe out the pan, add the remaining groundnut oil, the garlic and ginger and return to the medium heat.

As soon as the garlic begins to fizz, turn the heat up a notch and add the mushrooms. Stir-fry for about 5 minutes until browned. Add the miso, mirin, the remaining tablespoon of soy sauce and the soaked dried mushrooms with their broth, along with any reserved tofu marinade. Stir well until everything has dissolved, bring to the boil and simmer for about 3 minutes until the mushrooms are tender.

Divide the tofu between two warm serving bowls. Add the remaining tablespoon of sesame oil to the mushroom mixture off the heat and taste for seasoning – it shouldn't need anything, but you may wish to add a pinch of sugar to balance out the flavours. Ladle the hot mushroom broth over the tofu to serve. Finish with a sprig or two of coriander and a pile of delicate, crunchy sprouts, such as alfalfa or mustard.

THE HEARTY BEAN SOUP

Every cook needs a warming and hearty bean soup in their repertoire. This is the only one you need. This ultimate Tuscan-inspired soup has a slow-cooked base of sweet vegetables and garlic, borlotti beans and chickpeas, tomato, plenty of kale, bread to soak up the soup and fresh pesto to finish each bowl. As would be expected, the flavours and textures intensify and settle when the recipe is made ahead and reheated. Anoint each bowl with your best olive oil when eating.

In developing the soup, trying to hit on the perfect texture, I decided to soak and long-simmer dried borlotti beans for the deepest flavour and to retain their shape. The chickpeas, however, need to break down a little to add body. Cooking them from scratch is quite a bit of work so you'll see these are tinned. You could soak dried ones instead and simmer them separately, draining when tender and adding about 300g (10½oz) to the soup where the tinned are stirred in. A final note on vegetarian Parmesan rinds: save these when you get to the end of a wedge of cheese and keep in the freezer. They add extra umami to simmering soups and risottos and are simply removed at the end of cooking once they've done their job.

Serves 4 generously
Preparation time: 30 minutes, plus overnight soaking
Cooking time: 2 hours 30 minutes

4 tbsp olive oil
1 onion, chopped
2 large carrots, chopped
2 celery stalks, trimmed and chopped
2 leeks, trimmed and chopped
3 garlic cloves, crushed
½ tsp dried chilli (hot pepper) flakes
400g (14oz) tin of plum tomatoes
150g (5oz) cavolo nero, trimmed and thickly shredded
100g (3½oz) dried borlotti beans, soaked in plenty of cool water for 8–12 hours
400g (14oz) tin of chickpeas (garbanzos), drained
2 fresh or dried bay leaves
1 small vegetarian Parmesan rind (optional) (see intro)
a small bunch of flat-leaf parsley, stalks finely sliced, leaves chopped
sea salt and freshly ground black pepper

To serve
4 thick slices of stale sourdough or ciabatta bread
4 tbsp Summer Herb & Seed Pesto (page 175) or any fresh, ready-made pesto
the best extra virgin olive oil you have

Put 2 tablespoons of the olive oil in a large, sturdy, heatproof casserole (Dutch oven) or saucepan and place over a low heat. Add the onion with a pinch of salt and cook, stirring often, for about 7 minutes until it begins to soften. Add the chopped carrots, celery and leeks along with half the garlic and the chilli flakes and continue to cook for 5 minutes. Add the plum tomatoes and cavolo nero and cook for 5 minutes more, stirring frequently until the vegetables are soft and sweet and the tomatoes have begun to break down.

Add the drained, soaked borlotti beans, the tinned chickpeas, bay leaves and Parmesan rind (if using). Now pour in enough water to just cover the vegetables and bring to the boil. Cover with a lid and reduce the heat so that the soup putters very gently for 1 hour 30 minutes–2 hours until the beans are completely soft. Remove about a quarter of the soup mixture and mash or blend until smooth-ish. Return it to the pan to thicken the soup.

In a separate, small pan, warm the remaining 2 tablespoons of oil over a low heat and sauté the remaining garlic, along with the parsley stalks and leaves, for a couple of minutes until fragrant. Tip into the soup pan and stir in well. Remove the soup from the heat and leave to cool. Cover the pan and leave in the fridge for 12–24 hours for the flavours to develop.

When ready to eat, warm the uncovered soup through thoroughly over a low heat, stirring now and then. Add a little water if it seems too thick (remember this isn't a dainty soup) and season to taste. Sit a slice of bread in the bottom of each soup bowl and ladle the soup over. Finish with a spoonful of pesto and a drizzle of your best extra virgin olive oil.

BITTER LEAF SALAD WITH PEAR, GRAPE, BLUE CHEESE & HONEYED WALNUTS

An elegant salad to accompany a cheese board or something equally rich and intensely savoury, such as a fondue or vegetarian tart. Should you have some beautiful bread or some crisp crackers and a piquant blue cheese – a Roquefort, perhaps – they would make this salad a starter or small plate, rather than a side, as shown here.

Serves 4
Preparation time: 20 minutes
Cooking time: 30 minutes

For the honeyed walnuts
150g (5oz) walnut halves
100g (3½oz) floral honey
2 tsp thyme leaves

For the salad
300g (10½oz) black or red grapes
5 tbsp extra virgin olive oil, plus extra
    for oiling
2½ tbsp red wine vinegar
1½ tsp Dijon mustard
1 large ripe pear, halved and cored
1 tbsp lemon juice
2 large handfuls of bitter leaves, such
    as radicchio, chicory (Belgian
    endive) or frisée, separated or torn
    according to size
150g (5oz) Roquefort, crumbled
    (optional)
sea salt and freshly ground black
    pepper
good bread or crackers, to serve

To make the honeyed walnuts, preheat the oven to 170°C fan (190°C/375°F/gas 6) and oil a baking sheet.

Spread the walnut halves out on a second baking sheet and roast for about 6 minutes until golden.

Meanwhile, bring the honey, a large pinch of salt and 2 tablespoons of water to the boil in a small saucepan set over a high heat. Cook for 4–5 minutes until the honey syrup darkens to a deep amber colour. Add the toasted walnuts and the thyme leaves, stir well to coat, then spread out on the prepared tray and set aside to cool. Chop or bash into rough pieces.

Snip the grapes into smaller clusters of stalk (about 5 grapes per cluster). Space out on a baking sheet, brush with 1 tablespoon of the olive oil, season with salt and pepper and roast at the same temperature for 20 minutes until shrivelled and burst in places. Release from the tray with a spatula, moving the grapes closer to each other, and douse with 1 tablespoon of red wine vinegar while they're still hot.

Whisk the mustard, remaining 4 tablespoons of oil and remaining 1½ tablespoons of vinegar together to make a dressing. Taste and season with salt and pepper. It needs to be mustard-hot and sharp to contrast with the walnuts and grapes, but you can choose to sweeten it a little by crushing a couple of the roast grapes into it. Consider this trick if you will be including a strong blue cheese in the salad and need to balance it out.

Thinly slice the pear, then toss the pear slices with the lemon juice to prevent them browning. Tumble three-quarters of the dressing through the leaves, sliced pear and cheese, if using here. Serve on a platter or divided between smaller plates, adding the grapes and walnut pieces and drizzling with the reserved dressing either way. Accompany with good bread or crackers.

BEETROOT, WALNUT & HARISSA DIP

Use ready-cooked beetroots and a roasted pepper from a jar to dodge the initial cooking steps and simplify this recipe. I suppose this is essentially a version of the Levantine *muhammara*, a roasted red pepper, breadcrumb and walnut dip, but this smoother, sweet-sour beetroot incarnation has strayed quite far from the textured original. I often make it for wintery evenings as an alternative snack to hummus.

Serves 4 as a generous snack
Preparation time: 25 minutes
Cooking time: 1 hour
Vegan

3 medium beetroots (beets), scrubbed
1 red (bell) pepper
120g (4oz/scant 1¼ cups) walnut pieces
2 tsp cumin seeds
2 tsp chopped thyme leaves
1 garlic clove, crushed
2½ tbsp rose harissa, well stirred
3 tbsp extra virgin olive oil
juice of 1 lemon
1 tbsp pomegranate molasses
sea salt and freshly ground black
    pepper
8 slender slices of walnut rye bread,
    toasted, to serve

Preheat the oven to 180°C fan (200°C/400°F/gas 6).

Enclose each beetroot in a square of kitchen foil, making sure they are still wet from scrubbing. Place the parcels on a baking sheet and roast for about 50 minutes, or until completely tender when a skewer is inserted into the middle.

At the same time, put the pepper in a roasting tin and roast for about 30 minutes, turning halfway, until soft and charring all over. Tip into a bowl and cover with a plate so it steams as it cools. After 15 minutes or so, peel away the skin and discard the seeds and stalk, keeping the pepper flesh and any juices collected in the bowl.

Towards the end of cooking, spread the walnut halves out on a baking sheet and roast for about 6 minutes until lightly browned. Set aside.

Meanwhile, put the cumin seeds in a dry frying pan (skillet) set over a medium heat. Toast for 1–2 minutes, shaking the pan until fragrant and lightly toasted. Set aside.

Let the beetroots cool a little, then peel and roughly chop, making sure you wear protective gloves to prevent staining your fingers.

Roughly chop a tablespoon of toasted walnut pieces, combine with ½ teaspoon of toasted cumin seeds and 1 teaspoon of thyme leaves. Set aside.

Put the chopped beetroot in a food processor or high-speed blender with the roast pepper and its juices, the remaining toasted walnuts, toasted cumin seeds and thyme, the garlic, 2 tablespoons of harissa, the olive oil, the lemon juice and pomegranate molasses. Blend at high speed, stopping to scrape down the sides now and then.

This dip doesn't have to be perfectly smooth so keep some texture, if you like. Season to taste; it should be sweet, hot, sour and salty. You may wish to add more lemon juice or a dash more olive oil. Transfer to a serving bowl, topping with the remaining ½ tablespoon of harissa and the reserved chopped walnut mixture. Pile the toasted walnut rye bread alongside for dipping.

FIVE-SPICE SPRING ROLLS

A crisp-edged and lightly spiced spring roll is a marvellous thing and this will serve you well as a party recipe. Not particularly traditional, I'm afraid, but created in fond homage to a flavour memory; we would make something similar in my house as a child. Look out for the proper pastry wrappers in the freezer section of an East Asian food store. I'm all for using what you have to hand, but filo pastry won't really do here.

Any bought sriracha-type sauce will work as a dipping sauce instead of the Chinese black rice vinegar number detailed below. You could also combine a tablespoon of Tahini-Miso Sauce (page 182) with double the quantity of Kewpie mayonnaise to make an uncommonly delicious non-vegan alternative.

Makes about 20 spring rolls
Preparation time: 35 minutes,
plus 10 minutes cooling
Cooking time: 30 minutes
Vegan

60g (2oz) nest brown rice vermicelli
  noodles
2½ tbsp toasted sesame oil
a small thumb of ginger root, peeled
  and finely chopped
1 large garlic clove, finely chopped
1 tsp five-spice powder
450g (1lb) Chinese leaf cabbage (napa),
  cored and shredded
1 large carrot, finely shredded
170g (6oz) fresh beansprouts
a bunch of spring onions (scallions),
  trimmed and finely sliced
4 tbsp light soy sauce
2 tbsp Shaoxing rice wine
2 tbsp finely chopped garlic chives or
  standard chives
2 tbsp black rice vinegar (or use
  normal rice vinegar if unavailable)
1 red birdseye or Thai chilli,
  finely sliced
340g (12oz) pack 25 × 25cm (10 × 10in)
  pastry spring roll wrappers,
  defrosted
1.5 litres (56fl oz/6⅔ cups) groundnut
  (peanut) or vegetable oil, for
  deep-frying

Cover the rice noodles with cool water in a bowl and set aside for 15 minutes. Drain well; they should be pliable but not cooked.

Put 1½ tablespoons of the sesame oil in a large wok or frying pan (skillet) set over a high heat and add the ginger, garlic and five-spice. Fry for about 30 seconds until the garlic begins to sizzle but not colour. Add the cabbage, carrot and beansprouts and all but 1 tablespoon of the sliced spring onions, tossing to combine. Cook for 1–2 minutes until the cabbage begins to wilt. Add 2 tablespoons of soy sauce and the rice wine, reducing down briskly for 1–2 minutes so no liquid remains. Stir in the drained noodles and garlic chives or chives and stir-fry for a final few seconds to soften and combine. Remove from the heat and leave to cool in the pan for 10 minutes.

Meanwhile, make the dipping sauce if you wish to. In a small bowl, combine the remaining tablespoon of sesame oil and 2 tablespoons of soy sauce with the reserved sliced spring onions, the black rice vinegar and the sliced birdseye chilli. Set aside.

To fill the rolls, have a small bowl of water to hand and a large chopping board. Lay a spring roll wrapper on the board in a diamond shape, keeping the remaining wrappers covered with a damp tea (dish) towel. Place a heaped tablespoon of filling in the middle of the diamond and fold the bottom corner of the pastry halfway up towards the top corner. Now fold in the horizontal corners, first anointing them with a dab of water with your fingertip, then roll up towards the top to make a cigar shape, sealing the final top corner in place with another dab of water. Set the cigar aside on a tray, cover with a clean tea towel, and repeat the process to make about 20 rolls.

Turn your oven to its lowest setting and place a large baking sheet lined with paper towels in it. Put the oil for deep-frying in a large, deep, heavy-based saucepan; the oil should not reach more than halfway up the sides for safety. Have a platter lined with paper towels and a slotted spoon ready beside the stovetop. Set the pan over a low–medium heat and slowly heat the oil up to 180°C (350°F).

This will probably take longer than you think – reckon on 10 minutes or so. If you don't have a thermometer to check this, add a cube of white bread to the oil; it should turn golden in 30 seconds.

Adding them to the oil carefully and one by one, fry the shaped spring rolls in batches of 5–7. They should turn golden-brown and crisp in 6–8 minutes per batch. Stand over the pan and turn them over with your slotted spoon as they bob about to make sure they brown evenly. Use the slotted spoon to lift them out of the oil on to the lined platter, allowing them to drain, then transfer to the warm baking sheet. Return this to the low oven to keep warm while you cook the remaining rolls in the same way.

Serve the hot spring rolls with the dipping sauce – or another sauce of your choice.

ANY ROOT FRITTERS

These crisp-edged fritters should look raggedy and straggly, a bit like bhajis. You can vary the spices and herbs you add, having fun with spice mixes such as za'atar or chaat masala. The main point is you can use any root vegetables you like or need to use up. Choose non-watery, firm varieties such as parsnips, celeriac (celery root), sweet potato, carrots of all hues and golden, red or candy beetroots (beets) (you can use purple but their colour will bleed). Scrub or peel the root vegetables as needed, then finely shred or coarsely grate to use as the base of the batter. I have used the piquant Tarragon & Cornichon Aioli but you could use any characterful aioli or mayonnaise you love.

Serves 4 (makes about 20 fritters)
Preparation time: 20 minutes
Cooking time: 10 minutes

450g (1lb) root vegetables, shredded
    or coarsely grated (see intro)
1 small onion, halved and sliced
4 eggs
1 tsp ground turmeric
1½ tsp hot smoked paprika
a handful of flat-leaf parsley leaves,
    chopped
130–160g (4¼–5½oz/heaped
    1 cup–scant 1½ cups) chickpea
    (gram) flour
200–250ml (7–9fl oz/scant
    1 cup–1 cup) groundnut (peanut)
    oil, for deep-frying
a large handful of watercress sprigs,
    tough stalks removed
a drizzle of extra virgin olive oil
a squeeze of lemon juice
salt and freshly ground black pepper
100g (3½oz) drained cornichons,
    to serve
6 tbsp Tarragon & Cornichon Aioli
    (page 176)

Combine the shredded roots, onion, eggs, turmeric, paprika, parsley, 130g (4¼oz/heaped 1 cup) of the chickpea flour and a generous seasoning of salt and pepper in a large mixing bowl. If the mixture does not hold together as a thick batter, gradually add the remaining chickpea flour a teaspoon at a time until it just comes together and binds the vegetables. This will vary slightly depending on the roots used and their water content.

Turn the oven to its lowest setting to keep the cooked fritters warm as you work through the batches. Have ready a heatproof plate lined with paper towels.

Put 100ml (3½fl oz/scant ½ cup) of oil in a large, deep, heavy-based frying pan (skillet) set over a medium–high heat. Once shimmering – the surface should flicker and shake a little – gently lower in tablespoons of the batter, well spaced out, to make bhaji-like fritters. Cook no more than 6 very straggly fritters at a time.

Fry on each side for 2–3 minutes, flipping carefully halfway through, until golden and crisp all round. Use a slotted spoon to transfer them to the prepared plate, cover loosely with a sheet of kitchen foil and keep them warm in the oven. Repeat the fritter-cooking and draining process at least twice until all the batter is used, adding extra oil as needed. The number of batches it takes will depend on the size of your frying pan.

Toss the watercress sprigs with olive oil and lemon juice in a bowl, seasoning lightly with salt and pepper.

Serve the hot fritters with the dressed watercress leaves, cornichons and spoonfuls of the tarragon and cornichon aioli, or a similar aioli-style sauce.

ROAST PUMPKIN & PEPPER SOUP
WITH GRUYÈRE TOASTS & SMOKY SEEDS

Roasting vegetables as a soup base is a trick I can't resist. You'll find it used several times throughout this book and with good reason: not only does turning the oven on suit soup season, it is the easiest way I know to concentrate and caramelise the natural sugars in sweet vegetables and fruits such as onions, garlic, pumpkins and peppers. It would take such care and time to attain the same depth of flavour on a stovetop. Moreover, skins, peels and stalks can be quickly removed after cooking, keeping chopping time to a minimum. To achieve a velvet-smooth texture, blend the vegetables thoroughly and choose a dense-fleshed pumpkin or winter squash, such as Crown Prince, Kabocha or Golden Butternut.

Serves 4
Preparation time: 25 minutes
Cooking time: 1 hour

4½ tbsp olive oil
2 red onions, halved, skins left on
800g (1lb 12oz) dense-fleshed
   pumpkin or winter squash,
   deseeded and sliced into 4cm
   (2½in) thick wedges
2 red (bell) peppers, left whole
2 red chillies, left whole
4 garlic cloves, unpeeled
3–4 tiny thumbs of fresh turmeric,
   unpeeled
350ml (12¼fl oz/1½ cups) hot
   vegetable stock
30 sage leaves
4 tsp sunflower seeds
a large pinch of hot smoked paprika
4 thick diagonal slices of sourdough
   baguette
60g (2oz) Gruyère, finely grated
extra virgin olive oil, to drizzle
   (optional)
salt and freshly ground black pepper

Preheat the oven to 180°C fan (200°C/400°F/gas 6).

Drizzle 1 tablespoon of olive oil over the base of a large roasting tin, placing the halved onions in it, cut-sides down. Toss the pumpkin or squash slices and the whole red peppers in a further 2 tablespoons of oil and add to the pan, spacing out in a single layer. Roast for 30 minutes, then add the whole red chillies and unpeeled garlic and turmeric pieces, turning the squash and peppers over at the same time. Roast for about 20 minutes more until the vegetables are soft and slightly charred.

Cover the vegetables with kitchen foil or a baking sheet and leave to cool for 10 minutes. They will create steam and soften further. Peel the skins from the peppers and discard their stalks and seeds. Remove the stalks from the chillies, along with the skins if they pull away easily, plus the skins from the garlic cloves and halved onions. Scoop the flesh from the pumpkin or squash with a spoon to remove the skins. Don't be overly concerned about doing a perfect job here.

Transfer the peeled vegetables and any juices in the pan to a blender with the hot vegetable stock and blend until buttery-smooth. Season to taste with salt and pepper, then transfer to a saucepan and reheat gently over a low heat, stirring. This is meant to be a very thick soup but do add a little more stock or water if the consistency isn't to your liking.

While the soup is heating, pour 1 tablespoon of oil into a large frying pan (skillet) set over a low–medium heat and add two-thirds of the sage leaves. Fry for about 2–3 minutes until frazzled but not overly browned, turning the heat down if they crisp up too quickly. Tip onto a plate lined with paper towels and set aside.

Put a further ½ tablespoon of oil, the sunflower seeds and paprika in the same frying pan. Set over a medium heat and toast, stirring often, for a couple of minutes until the seeds turn golden. Season with salt and pepper, tip onto the plate with the sage leaves and set aside.

Preheat the grill to medium–high and toast the bread slices on a baking sheet for about 3 minutes until lightly browned on top. Flip the slices over. Finely slice the remaining sage leaves and combine with the grated Gruyère. Divide between the bread slices. Season with black pepper, then grill for about 4 minutes until the cheese is melted and bubbling.

Divide the hot soup between warmed serving bowls and immediately top with the cheese toasts, scattering with the crisp sage leaves and smoky sunflower seeds. Add a few drops of extra virgin olive oil and a twist of black pepper to finish, if liked.

SUPPER

This is a chapter of proper food: big plates or satisfying suppers with that bit more swagger. I've kept sustenance and, often, entertaining in mind, as I still hear people say they find making satisfying or well-balanced vegetarian main courses a challenge.

Swagger doesn't mean stress. Where the nature of the recipe allows, textures and flavours will settle after slow and careful cooking – or an overnight stint in the fridge – before reheating if and when needed. This is only to your advantage when cooking for friends or family so, much like the final, desserts chapter, I have endeavoured to make many of these 'bigger' recipes conducive to advance groundwork. In these cases, everything will be done in advance and, because you will have tasted it, you can relax in the knowledge that supper is sure to be delicious.

On this note, it often baffles me that so many of us will have sat in a restaurant, with calm chefs in an open kitchen putting their *mise en place* together in front of our fascinated eyes. Yet we presume we should be able to produce complex food for celebratory meals in the evenings, probably after a long day at work, with not even an onion chopped before starting. This isn't how professional chefs cook, so why some home cooks place that kind of expectation on themselves is beyond me. If you are short on time, have the confidence to choose one of the many simple salads or other relaxed recipes elsewhere in the book – whatever appeals – and serve it with good bread and cheese.

If you do want to push the boat out, the pleasingly retro Big Green Tart, filled with goats' cheese and vegetables, is enjoyable to make but undeniably a project, so it's one to make ahead and serve with dressed leaves. Similarly, the Mushroom, Pumpkin & Chestnut Claypot, a light stew based on Vietnamese flavours, will improve so much if made ahead, as will a truly Excellent Ratatouille or the Baked Stuffed Tomatoes.

A few of the modern-classic-worthy recipes are designed to be thrown together as needed. A lavish but light Thai-inspired papaya salad, an exceptionally good aubergine curry inspired by the flavours of Kerala (one of my absolute favourites in this book) or the most chicest of mushroom pastas for a romantic two all fall into this category.

I've woven in many tricks so that you can appear organised and collected, regardless of whether these suppers are made on the night or you've spent an hour or two cooking the previous evening with a favourite podcast on. In the latter case, your future ratatouilles and Imam Bayaldi aubergines will thank you.

RISOTTO WITH ROAST RADICCHIO
& BLACK OLIVE CRUMB

Radicchio's gentle bitterness is rounded out by caramelizing it in the oven to adorn a simply perfect risotto. Crisp and rustic, black olive breadcrumbs add texture. Be delicate when cooking the rice, stirring in one direction as the Italians do and aiming for the just-tender rice to 'flow' across the plate, rather than sitting in a sticky, dry clag. The resting time in the pan at the end is essential, as is having everyone seated at the table, ready and waiting to eat.

Serves 4
Preparation time: 30 minutes
Cooking time: 1 hour 20 minutes

80g (3oz) stale sourdough or ciabatta
80g (3oz) black olives, stoned and
　　roughly chopped
5½ tbsp olive oil
8 young rosemary tips
4 chicory (Belgian endive), halved,
　　or radicchio, cut into wedges
1 tbsp good balsamic vinegar
1 litre (34fl oz/4 cups) good-quality
　　vegetable stock
50g (1¾oz) unsalted butter
1 sweet white onion, finely chopped
275g (9½oz/1¼ cups) Carnaroli
　　risotto rice
150ml (5fl oz/scant ⅔ cup) dry white
　　wine
50g (1¾oz) vegetarian Parmesan,
　　finely grated, plus extra to serve
1 heaped tbsp crème fraîche
sea salt and freshly ground black
　　pepper

Preheat the oven to 170°C fan (190°C/375°F/gas 5).

To make the olive crumb, blitz the bread pieces in a food processor until they form quite fine crumbs, adding the chopped olives halfway through so they end up in larger pieces.

Combine 1½ tablespoons of the olive oil with these breadcrumbs, seasoning with salt and pepper. Spread them out on a baking sheet, pushing them towards one side. Combine the tiny rosemary sprigs with a further tablespoon of the oil and scatter into the gap alongside the crumbs. Roast for 8–10 minutes until golden and crisp, stirring the crumbs halfway and checking the rosemary sprigs at that point, removing them if they are browned. Set aside to cool. The crisp crumbs can be made a couple of days ahead and kept in an airtight container in a cool place.

To cook the chicory or radicchio wedges, coat them with 2 tablespoons of olive oil. Nestle in a roasting tin, season with salt and pepper, then roast for 30 minutes or so, turning over halfway, until caramelised and softened. Sprinkle the vinegar over, turning to coat, then set aside.

Meanwhile, put the stock in a medium saucepan and bring to the boil. Reduce the heat to a very gentle simmer and have a ladle ready.

Melt 20g (¾oz) of the butter and 1 tablespoon of the olive oil in a deep-sided frying pan (skillet) and add the onion. Cook over a low heat for 10 minutes, stirring often, until soft and sweet but not coloured.

Increase the heat slightly and add the rice, stirring to coat it in the butter for about a minute until the grains appear translucent. Pour the wine into the pan, allowing it to evaporate to almost nothing, then add a ladle of hot stock and begin to gently stir the rice in one direction. Cook until the stock is absorbed. Add another ladle of stock and stir as before, repeating the process for around 18 minutes until the rice is tender but retains a good bite in the middle. The risotto should be on the loose side, flowing in texture. Remove from the heat, stir in half the vegetarian Parmesan, the remaining butter and the crème fraîche. Season to taste with salt and pepper and re-cover with a lid for 5 minutes.

Divide the risotto among four shallow bowls, nestling the roast radicchio in the middle. Scatter with the rosemary leaves, olive crumb and extra grated Parmesan, offering more of the latter two alongside.

BAKED DOLMADES WITH BEETROOT TZATZIKI

A neon-purple herb and beetroot tzatziki livens up these spiced courgette, walnut, lentil, dried apricot, herb and rice dolmades. It's a project of a recipe, but perfect for bringing sunshine to a kitchen on a grey day. Ideally, you'd make the dolmades ahead so that their flavours develop, then serve cold or at room temperature with salad, warmed flatbreads and the dayglo tzatziki.

Serves 6 (makes about 40 dolmades)
Preparation time: 1 hour
Cooking time: 2 hours

For the dolmades
150g (5oz/heaped ⅔ cup) brown
    short-grain rice
1 lemon
about 300g (10½oz) large vine leaves
    in brine (about 50 leaves), drained
50g (1¾oz/½ cup) walnuts, finely
    chopped
1 large onion, finely chopped
1 small courgette (zucchini), finely
    chopped
1 small carrot, finely chopped
about 200ml (7fl oz/scant 1 cup) extra
    virgin olive oil
1 garlic clove, crushed
30g (1oz/scant ¼ cup) dried apricots,
    finely chopped
400g (14oz) tin of green lentils, rinsed
    and drained
¼ tsp ground allspice
a small bunch of dill fronds,
    finely chopped
a small bunch of mint leaves,
    finely chopped
a small bunch of flat-leaf parsley
    leaves, finely chopped

For the tzatziki
300g (10½oz/1¼ cups) strained
    Greek yogurt or labneh
1 large garlic clove, crushed
1 medium beetroot (beet), peeled
    and coarsely grated
2 tbsp pomegranate arials
sea salt and freshly ground
    black pepper

Rinse the rice, then cover with plenty of cool water and leave to soak for 1 hour. Grate the lemon zest, then slice the lemon as finely as possible to make about 8 rounds in total.

Blanch the vine leaves in a large saucepan of boiling water for 3 minutes. Tip into a colander in the sink and refresh under cool water, draining well.

Place the walnuts in a large frying pan (skillet) and toast over a medium heat, shaking the pan often, for a few minutes until fragrant and lightly browned. Set aside.

In a large saucepan with a lid, fry the onion, courgette, carrot and a pinch of salt in 2–3 tablespoons of olive oil for about 10 minutes. The salt will help the vegetables to release their water and gently caramelise. Stir the vegetables often until they are very soft but not highly coloured. Drain the rice and add it to the pan with another tablespoon or so of olive oil. Cook over a low heat for another 12–15 minutes until the rice grains begin to look translucent. Remove from the heat, tip into a bowl and add the lemon zest, walnuts, garlic, apricots, lentils and allspice with two-thirds each of the dill, mint and parsley. Season generously with salt and pepper.

Reserve the remaining herbs for the tzatziki and finishing the dish. It's fine to mix them all together at this stage, cover and keep chilled.

To fill the dolmades, lay a drained vine leaf out flat, vein-side up. Place a heaped teaspoon of the rice mixture at the stalk end of the leaf. Fold over the bottom of the leaf to just cover the mixture. Now fold in the sides of the leaf and roll up to form a chubby cigar. Repeat to use up all the filling and leaves, making about 40 dolmades.

Preheat the oven to 170°C fan (190°C/375°F/gas 5).

Lay most of the remaining vine leaves over the bottom of a heavy-based dish – about 25cm (10in) square is ideal – letting them overhang all around the edges. Set 5 large leaves aside for later. Add your first layer of stuffed vine leaves to the dish, packing them in so they are fairly snug. Put a couple of lemon slices on top, then begin with another layer of the stuffed vine leaves. Continue until all the rolls are packed in, adding a final few lemon slices to finish. Pour in 200ml (7fl oz/scant 1 cup) of water and the remaining 150ml (5fl oz/scant ⅔ cup) of olive oil. Lay the few remaining vine leaves on top, laid out flat, bringing in all the overlapping leaves around the edges.

Cover the dish with kitchen foil, tucking it around tightly, and sit a weight, such as a heavy pan, on top. Bake for 1 hour 30 minutes, or until the dolmades are tender throughout when the point of a knife is inserted.

Once cooked, leave to rest for a minimum of 20 minutes, preferably more like 45 minutes if you have the time. The dolmades will firm up as they cool. Uncover and serve warm. Alternatively, keep chilled and eat them cold or at room temperature up to 5 days later.

To make the tzatziki, combine most of the reserved chopped herbs with the strained yogurt, garlic and beetroot and season to taste with salt and pepper. Transfer to a small serving bowl and scatter with pomegranate arials and any remaining chopped herbs. Serve the dolmades with the bright-purple tzatziki alongside.

EXCELLENT RATATOUILLE

This is the ratatouille to put all others in the shade but, make no mistake, it doesn't claim to be traditional in method. I'm making the most of the oven to caramelise sweet, late-summer vegetables separately (as you might a shallow roasted-vegetable *tian*), later cloaking them in the lightest of summer tomato sauces with plenty of basil and really good olive oil. Don't stint on the latter; it has an essential role adding joy and flavour. Make sure your vegetables are very chunky – cut in big diagonal slices – so they keep their shapes as much as possible.

You need to make any ratatouille at least a day ahead. The flavours will mellow and the textures, particularly those of the melting courgettes and aubergine, settle into the sauce. If you have big enough pans, double the recipe and eat the results over the next week or so.

Serve in bountiful portions – I have been particularly generous here, but it's an easy dish to eat a lot of – drizzled with extra virgin olive oil, scattered with basil leaves and accompanied by spoonfuls of Basil & Lemon Pistou (page 180). You'll need a warm, crusty sourdough baguette on the table with a bowlful of plump haricot beans, again dressed with a little of the same pistou and more extra virgin olive oil.

Serves 4-6, but easily doubled
Preparation time: 50 minutes
Cooking time: 1 hour
Vegan

about 8 tbsp extra virgin olive oil,
    plus extra to serve
2 large aubergines (eggplants),
    halved and thickly sliced
3 small red onions, sliced
4 thyme sprigs, leaves stripped
4 medium courgettes (zucchini),
    thickly sliced diagonally
4 large red (bell) peppers, deseeded
    and cut into large chunks
2 large garlic cloves, left unpeeled

For the tomato sauce
1kg (2lb 4oz) flavourful plum
    tomatoes, preferably San Marzano
2 large garlic cloves, crushed
3 oregano sprigs, leaves stripped
5 tbsp extra virgin olive oil, plus extra
    to serve
a handful of basil leaves, torn or
    chopped, plus extra to serve
sea salt and freshly ground
    black pepper

Pistou or pesto, bread and dressed
    white beans, to serve (see intro)

Start by roasting the vegetables. Preheat the oven to 180°C fan (200°C/400°F/gas 6). Have two large roasting tins ready; it's pivotal that the vegetables have space to caramelise properly in single layers in the oven or they will steam and turn soft. Drizzle both pans with a little olive oil to coat the surface. Lay the aubergines and sliced onions out in a single layer in one pan. Scatter with half the thyme leaves and and drizzle generously with olive oil, seasoning well with salt and pepper. Repeat the same process in the second pan with the courgettes and red peppers, then tucking an unpeeled garlic clove underneath the vegetables in each pan so they are protected from scorching. Roast both pans for about 45 minutes until the vegetables are soft and browned at the edges but still holding their shapes. Set aside to cool for a few minutes. Using a spatula and being careful not to crush them too much, transfer one lot of vegetables to the pan with the others. Peel the soft garlic cloves, crushing their sweet flesh and returning it to the pan.

Meanwhile, to make the tomato sauce, first skin the tomatoes. Make a shallow cross in the base of each with a knife and place in a large, heatproof bowl. Boil a full kettle and pour the boiling water over to cover the tomatoes generously. Leave for 1 minute, then fish out a tomato with a slotted spoon and check if the skin is peeling and pulling away easily from the base. If not, return to the bowl and leave for another minute before draining. The trick is to catch them before the flesh starts to soften, meaning just the fragile skins peel off without taking a layer of flavour with them. Chop the flesh very roughly, not bothering to deseed, and transfer the tomatoes and juice to a medium saucepan as you go.

Add the crushed garlic, oregano leaves and 2 tablespoons of olive oil to the saucepan. Place over a low heat and bring up to a gentle simmer. Season lightly with salt and pepper and cook down for

20 minutes, stirring until the tomatoes are sauce-y but retain quite a bit of their texture. Now spoon this tomato mixture over the vegetables in their single pan and sprinkle with the torn basil. This is your ratatouille, so check the seasoning and drizzle with a little more oil for flavour. If the pan won't fit in your fridge, carefully transfer to one that will. Ideally you'd chill it overnight and gently reheat the following day or the day after that. I find it easiest to do this in the original foil-covered tin in a moderate oven.

Serve at room temperature or warm, drizzled with more oil and scattered with extra basil leaves. As per the introduction, accompany with pistou or a pesto, bread and dressed white beans.

TOFU BAO BUNS

Track down frozen bao buns in the frozen section of an East Asian food store and fill them with this addictive mix of roast tofu, pickled cucumber, spring onions, sesame mayonnaise and crushed cashews. You'll need to make the undiluted Tahini-Miso Sauce for this, but it takes less than 5 minutes so it shouldn't be too much of a bind.

Makes 8 buns
Preparation time: 30 minutes
Cooking time: 40 minutes

300g (10½oz) extra-firm tofu,
    drained and sliced into 8
2 tbsp soy sauce
1 tbsp honey
1 tbsp finely grated ginger root
½ tsp five-spice powder
½ tsp chilli (hot pepper) flakes
2 tbsp toasted sesame oil
½ large cucumber, sliced
2 tbsp mirin
2 tsp unrefined caster (superfine)
    sugar
2 tbsp rice vinegar
3 tbsp Kewpie mayonnaise or mayo
    of your choice
2 tbsp Tahini-Miso Sauce (page 182)
8 frozen bao buns
3 spring onions (scallions),
    finely shredded
a small handful of coriander (cilantro)
    sprigs
100g (3½oz/⅔ cup) salted roasted
    cashews, crushed
sriracha sauce and Pickled Carrots,
    drained (page 182), to serve

Preheat the oven to 200°C fan (220°C/425°F/gas 7).

Toss the tofu in a roasting tin with the soy, honey, ginger, five-spice, half the chilli flakes and the sesame oil. Roast for 20 minutes, turning halfway with a spatula, until glazed and browned.

Meanwhile, put the cucumber in a bowl. Put the remaining chilli flakes in a small saucepan with the mirin, sugar, rice vinegar and 2 tablespoons of water. Bring to the boil, then simmer briskly until the liquid is reduced to about 3 tablespoons. Pour over the sliced cucumber and set aside for 10 minutes before eating, or cover and chill for up to 5 days.

In a separate bowl, combine the mayonnaise with the tahini-miso sauce.

Set a large pan of water over a medium heat and bring to the boil. Set a lidded steamer, preferably bamboo and in two tiers, on top. Arrange the frozen buns in the steamer baskets, spaced at least 2cm (¾in) apart, and steam – not too fiercely – for 10–12 minutes, or according to the pack instructions. Once done, they will be puffed, shiny and springy to the touch.

Split the warm buns open, removing their inner papers, and fill with a little tahini-miso-mayo, the roast tofu slices, pickled cucumber, shredded spring onions, sprigs of coriander and lots of crushed cashews for texture. You can also offer sriracha chilli sauce and pickled carrots alongside, plus the extra tahini-miso-mayo.

KERALA-STYLE AUBERGINE & TOMATO CURRY

The flavours here – fresh and true – are inspired by beautiful Keralan curries. If you think of a curry as a rich or heavy dish, try this and think again. The sauce is delicate and light, but if you do want to add extra richness, pour a little coconut cream into the simmered tomatoes. To my mind, the flavours shine better without.

If you can find long blue-purple Chinese aubergines, use them here. They are the perfect shape for this curry, their thin skins holding together with innards turning silken. You'll need to cut them into 5cm long cylinders and not be perturbed if their former purple hue takes on slightly green tones after roasting. Failing this, slender versions of standard dark-purple aubergines are fine, simply halve them from top to bottom before slicing into thick half-moons. Roasting is an essential step to add caramel flavours and a melting texture – the disappointment of an undercooked aubergine is all too real – and the curry itself comes together in no time afterwards.

Serves 4 in delicate portions
Preparation time: 25 minutes
Cooking time: 45 minutes

4 slender, long aubergines (eggplants),
   sliced into 5cm (2in) cylinders or
   4 slender standard aubergines,
   halved and cut into very thick
   half-moons
3 tbsp groundnut (peanut) oil
5 large plum tomatoes
4 large eggs
1 sweet white onion, chopped
2 tsp brown mustard seeds
2 curry leaf sprigs, stripped
1 red chilli, finely chopped
2 mild green chillies, 1 finely chopped,
   1 finely sliced
2 tsp finely chopped fresh turmeric
1 tbsp finely chopped ginger root
2 garlic cloves, finely chopped
a handful of coriander (cilantro)
   sprigs
sea salt and freshly ground
   black pepper
2 tbsp crisp fried onions, to serve
steamed brown rice, to serve

Preheat the oven to 170°C fan (190°C/375°F/gas 5).

Coat the aubergine cylinders or pieces with half the oil, spread them out in a roasting tin and season with salt and pepper. Roast for 25 minutes until turning golden and just tender.

Skin the tomatoes. Make a shallow cross in the base of each with a knife and place in a large heatproof bowl. Boil a kettle and pour the boiling water over to cover generously. Leave for 1 minute, then fish out a tomato with a slotted spoon and check if the skin is peeling and pulling away easily from the base. If not, return to the bowl and leave for another minute before draining. The trick is to catch them before the flesh starts to soften, meaning just the fragile skins peel off without taking a layer of flavour with them. Chop the flesh very roughly, including the seeds, and set aside.

Soft-boil the eggs by covering with cold water in a saucepan, bringing to the boil, then immediately turning the heat off and leaving for 7 minutes. Refresh under cool water, drain and carefully peel.

In a large wok or wide frying pan (skillet) set over a low–medium heat, fry the onion and a pinch of salt in a further tablespoon of the oil for around 7 minutes, until softened. Add 1 teaspoon of the mustard seeds and fry until they begin to sputter, then stir in half the curry leaves with the chopped chilli, turmeric, ginger and garlic. Fry for about 5 minutes. Add the chopped tomatoes and cook down for a few minutes more until thickened. There should be plenty of tomato texture remaining. Fold in the roast aubergine and season to taste with salt and pepper. Once simmering, nestle the halved soft-boiled eggs on top to warm though, keeping their yolk-sides facing up.

To finish, put a small frying pan over a medium heat with the remaining ½ tablespoon of oil. Add the remaining teaspoon of mustard seeds, green chilli and sprig of curry leaves, cooking for about 2 minutes until they splutter and begin to crisp. Spoon the curry into serving bowls and spoon over the tempered spices, offering coriander sprigs and crisp onions to scatter over, with steamed rice on the side.

MUSHROOM PACCHERI WITH BROWNED BUTTER & THYME

Silky browned thyme butter, layers of mushroom umami, garlic … Try to make this luxurious pasta when interesting and flavourful woodland mushrooms are in season. Either sliced porcini or the similar king oyster are a must for their firm texture; chanterelles, pied de mouton, sliced chestnut and oyster mushrooms are all fine additions.

Serves 2
Preparation time: 20 minutes
Cooking time: 30 minutes

15g (½oz) dried porcini mushrooms
1 tsp white miso
40g (1½oz) unsalted butter
2 tsp chopped thyme leaves
½ tbsp olive oil
160g (5½oz) dried paccheri pasta
2 garlic cloves, finely chopped
300g (10½oz) mixed woodland
    mushrooms, sliced or torn
    according to size and type
    (see intro)
5 tbsp dry white wine
4 tbsp finely grated vegetarian
    Parmesan or Pecorino, plus extra
    to serve
freshly ground black pepper

Cover the dried mushrooms and the miso with 4 tablespoons of boiling water. Set aside for 10 minutes, then drain.

Melt the butter in a large frying pan (skillet) set over a low–medium heat until foaming. Cook, stirring often, for a few minutes until beginning to brown and smell 'nutty'. Once the milk solids in the butter turn a caramel colour and it looks amber, add the thyme and olive oil and remove from the heat.

Cook the pasta according to the pack instructions until on the al dente side of al dente, then drain, reserving some of the starchy cooking water in a mug.

As the pasta cooks, add both the fresh and the drained dried mushrooms to the thyme butter and sauté over a medium–high heat for about 5–7 minutes until the fresh mushrooms are tender and deeply golden at the edges. Add the mushroom-miso water and the wine to the pan and cook for a further 2 minutes, bubbling the mixture down to thicken it a little. Toss in the drained paccheri with a few tablespoons of cooking water, tossing through in the pan. Add the grated Parmesan or Pecorino and continue to flip the pan over the gentle heat to make a silky, emulsified sauce coating the just-tender pasta. Season with black pepper and serve straight away, with extra grated cheese, if liked.

THAI-INSPIRED GREEN PAPAYA, MANGO & TOFU SALAD

The challenge of emulating the umami of Thai shrimp paste and the like with vegan and vegetarian-friendly ingredients is greatly enjoyable. They aren't traditional, but in this delectable, Thai-style salad – based on the famous Som Tam or green papaya salad – sundried tomato and miso pastes offer much of the savoury depth required. You'll need a pestle and mortar to make it effectively and a shredding tool (like a vegetable peeler but with little teeth) will make light work of the green papaya.

If you can only buy tamarind in a sticky block (superior in taste compared to the jarred paste), soak 90g (3¼oz) of tamarind in 90ml (3fl oz/generous ⅓ cup) of boiling water for 10 minutes before mashing with a fork and pushing through a sieve. Stir well before using.

Makrut limes are knobbly, fragranced citrus, native to Southeast Asia. The magic lies in their zest and their leaves, which are intensely perfumed. The latter are pretty easy to track down, depending on where you live, but don't worry too much about the limes themselves, unless you live near an excellent Southeast Asian food store; standard limes are not the same, but will do.

Serves 4
Preparation time: 30 minutes
Vegan

4 garlic cloves, roughly chopped
10 cherry tomatoes, halved
1 tbsp miso paste
1 tbsp sundried tomato purée (paste)
3–4 tiny birdseye or scud Thai chillies, stalks removed
90g (3¼oz) fine green beans, trimmed and cut into 4cm (2½in) lengths
5 tbsp crushed roasted peanuts
1 slice makrut lime or normal lime
2 small green papaya, peeled and finely shredded, leaving the seeds behind
70g (2¼oz) crushed palm sugar or light muscovado sugar
90ml (3fl oz/generous ⅓ cup) lime juice
90ml (3fl oz/generous ⅓ cup) tamarind water (see intro)
4 tbsp vegan 'fish' sauce
¼ tsp chilli powder
1 ripe mango, peeled, pitted and sliced
200g (7oz) smoked almond tofu, drained and sliced
a handful of Thai basil leaves
sea salt

Crush the garlic with a pinch of sea salt flakes in a pestle and mortar until it forms a smooth paste. Transfer to a mixing bowl, then use the pestle and mortar to lightly crush the halved tomatoes. Add to the bowl with the garlic.

Now crush the miso, sundried tomato purée and 3 of the chillies together until the chillies are roughly pounded. Add the beans, half the peanuts and the lime slice, then pound again until the beans appear crushed in places.

Add the papaya to the bean mixture and pound again to lightly bruise and tenderise. Tip everything into the garlic bowl with the palm sugar, lime juice, tamarind water, vegan 'fish' sauce and chilli powder. Combine thoroughly then taste; the salad should be hot, salty, sweet and sour so adjust the lime juice, sugar, salt or the final chilli (crush first), if needed. Remove the lime slice before tumbling the sliced mango, smoked tofu and basil leaves through the mixture.

Serve on a platter, scattered with the remaining crushed peanuts.

MUSHROOM, PUMPKIN & CHESTNUT CLAYPOT

It's unheard of for a claypot to include any roasting steps – they would be cooked over a flame by their very nature – but this caramelising step adds swagger to the vegetables with little extra work and means their simmering time can be controlled, keeping the flavours of the stew bright and the textures intact. The warming spices and sweet-salty broth is inspired by North Vietnam, where there is plenty of Chinese influence. Make it a day ahead and gently reheat, if you can. Eat the stew with brown rice, Fragrant Chilli Oil (page 172) (or any crispy chilli oil), steamed greens and wholegrain rice. You could add cubes of firm tofu to the simmering vegetables to absorb some of the broth and increase the protein in this dish.

Serves 4
Preparation time: 25 minutes
Cooking time: 1 hour 10 minutes
Vegan

1.1kg (2lb 5 oz) golden butternut squash or dense-fleshed pumpkin, deseeded and peeled if liked, and cut into chubby wedges
4 small or banana shallots (echalions), halved
4 tbsp groundnut (peanut) oil
250g (9oz) mixed mushrooms, such as shiitake or king oyster, thickly sliced
4 large garlic cloves, sliced
25g (1oz) ginger root, peeled and sliced into thin coins
1 red chilli, pierced but left whole
25g (1oz) palm sugar or light muscovado sugar
2 whole star anise
1 small cinnamon stick
180g (6¼oz) vacuum-packed whole chestnuts
4 tbsp vegan 'fish' sauce or light soy sauce
300ml (10fl oz/1¼ cups) unsweetened coconut water (not coconut milk)
1 tbsp toasted sesame oil
sea salt and freshly ground black pepper

To serve
lime wedges
2 spring onions (scallions), finely shredded
a handful of coriander (cilantro) leaves

Preheat the oven to 180°C fan (200°C/400°F/gas 6).

Toss the squash or pumpkin with the shallots and 2 tablespoons of the oil. Season with salt and pepper and spread out in a large roasting tin big enough to hold the vegetables in a single layer. Make sure the shallot halves are sitting cut-sides down. Roast for 45 minutes, carefully turning halfway, until caramelised and tender.

Meanwhile, toss the sliced mushrooms with a further tablespoon of oil on a large baking sheet. Spread out so they're not touching and season well with salt and pepper. Roast at the top of the oven for about 20 minutes until browned.

Meanwhile, put the remaining tablespoon of oil in a large flameproof casserole (Dutch oven) or heavy-based saucepan set over a low heat. Add the garlic, ginger and whole chilli, frying gently for a couple of minutes to soften but not colour. Add the sugar and caramelise for 1–2 minutes, stirring in the star anise and cinnamon stick just before the sugar begins to catch. Add the chestnuts, vegan 'fish' sauce and coconut water, simmering down for 5 minutes. Now carefully transfer the roasted vegetables to the pan and cover it with a lid. Simmer very gently for about 20 minutes to cook out the aromatics but not over-do the vegetables.

If possible, make this ahead of time and allow to cool in the pan, then chill overnight, reheating gently when needed. Be aware of the whole chilli, star anise and cinnamon stick when serving; they look pretty but won't be great to bite down on. Before plating up, drizzle with toasted sesame oil and check the seasoning. The flavours will be intense even though the broth is thin, but if it seems too salty for you, add a squeeze of lime from the wedges you'll have to hand.

Ladle over steamed brown rice in bowls, accompany with steamed or stir-fried greens and finish with shredded spring onion and coriander. Offer chilli oil and the lime wedges to squeeze over, if liked.

BIG GREEN TART

A handsome, celebratory tart of roast broccoli and tomatoes, goats' cheese and herbs with a buttery and short cumin pastry. You could top or accompany this with a pretty Delicate Cress & Herb Salad with Shallot & Radish. If you don't want to make your own pastry (and though this thyme and cumin seed version is excellent, I wouldn't blame you; it's a dying art these days and does take time), use 300g (10½oz) all-butter shortcrust, blind baking as below.

Serves 6 generously
Preparation time: 1 hour 20 minutes, plus 30 minutes chilling
Cooking time: 1 hour 15 minutes

1 tsp cumin seeds
100g (3½oz/heaped ¾ cup) plain (all-purpose) flour
70g (2¼oz/½ cup) buckwheat flour
¼ tsp salt
2½ tbsp chopped thyme leaves
75g (2½oz) unsalted butter, chilled and diced
2–3 tbsp iced water
300g (10½oz) tenderstem broccoli spears
300g (10½oz) cherry tomatoes
2 tbsp olive oil
300g (10½oz) goats' cheese log with skin, sliced 2cm (½in) thick
4 large eggs
450g (1lb) crème fraîche
25g (1oz) basil leaves, roughly chopped
sea salt and freshly ground black pepper
Delicate Cress & Herb Salad with Shallot & Radish (page 161), to serve

To make the pastry, first toast the cumin seeds in a dry frying pan (skillet) set over a medium heat for 1–2 minutes until fragrant. Crush roughly and set aside.

Use a balloon whisk to whisk the flours and salt together in a large bowl. This is the lazy way to sift and aerate the flour. Add the cumin seeds, ½ tablespoon of chopped thyme and the butter and, using a blunt knife, begin to cut the fat into the flour until it's finely chopped in. Go in with cool, clean hands and lightly rub the fat into the flour, lifting it up high and allowing it to drop back into the bowl to aerate it further. It should resemble rough sand. Sprinkle in 1 tablespoon of iced water, then, with a knife, start forming the dough as you sprinkle teaspoons of water over, using the knife at first until it begins to cling together. Once claggy, discard the knife and bring it together with your fingertips. When enough water has been added, the pastry should leave the bowl fairly clean. The quantity of water you need will vary with the flour you use, so only add it gradually. Knead very briefly until smooth, then form into a disc, wrap in clingfilm (plastic wrap) and chill for 30 minutes to rest.

Meanwhile, preheat the oven to 180°C fan (200°C/400°F/gas 6).

Drizzle the tenderstem broccoli and tomatoes with 2 tablespoons of oil in a roasting tin and season well with salt and pepper. Roast for 20 minutes until the broccoli is frazzled and tender and the tomatoes bursting. Set aside.

Beat all 4 eggs together in a large bowl and remove a tablespoon to a cup to use to seal the pastry. Add the crème fraîche, most of the basil and most of the remaining thyme leaves to the eggs in the bowl and season generously with salt and pepper, mixing well. Chill until needed.

Turn the oven to 160°C fan (180°C/350°F/gas 4).

On a lightly floured surface, roll the pastry disc out to a circle of 27cm (10¾in) diameter. Use to line a 6–7cm (2½in) deep, 23cm (9in) diameter tart tin with a removable base, letting the edges of the pastry overhang. Prick the base all over with a fork. Place a large sheet of non-stick baking parchment on top of the pastry and fill the middle with baking beans, raw pulses or uncooked rice to weigh the pastry down and keep it in place. Bake for 20 minutes, then carefully remove the paper and beans. Continue to cook the uncovered tart for about 10 minutes more until pale golden and sandy-looking. Immediately paint the base and insides of the hot pastry with the reserved beaten egg to seal any gaps. Trim the excess edges flush with the tin using a sharp knife (I find serrated best). The cooked case can be kept in a sealed container in a cool place for a few days at this stage, if needed.

Turn the oven down to 150°C fan (170°C/340°F/gas 3).

Sit the tart case on a large baking sheet. Carefully fill it with the herb custard, roast broccoli, cherry tomatoes and goats' cheese, finishing with a few slices of goats' cheese on top and scattering with the reserved herb leaves. Bake in the middle of the oven for about 50–60 minutes until risen, golden and just set in the middle. Leave to cool for at least 15 minutes to firm up the pastry and custard before removing from the tart tin. Serve warm or at room temperature with dressed salad leaves or, ideally, with the herb salad with shallot and radish.

BLACK BEAN CHILLI

No sweet and sickly bean stews here; this is a black bean chilli with real character, long-simmered and sonorous with smoky dried chillies. Make this at least a day ahead and serve it reheated in tacos or baked sweet potatoes with crushed avocado, coriander, jalapeño chillies and lime. Or do as I have suggested and brighten it up with a Chimichurri sauce, quinoa, salad and sour cream. Miss out any dairy serving suggestions to keep the recipe vegan.

Remember to begin this recipe ahead of time by soaking the dried black beans for 8 hours or overnight before cooking. Otherwise, use 500g (12lb 2oz) drained weight of cooked black beans.

You will need smoky, shiny dried chillies to make this and I'm afraid they may be easiest to procure online if you don't live near a good spice shop or Mexican grocer. (In the UK, www.coolchile.co.uk sells them.) For balance and the requisite heat, a couple of tiny, hot zingers, such as arbol or cascabel will turn the temperature up. Sweeter, milder chillies, such as the New Mexico variety I have suggested, are then backed up by the whomp of a rich and fruity type, such as ancho, mulato or pasilla.

Serves 8
Preparation time: 40 minutes, plus overnight soaking
Cooking time: 2 hours
Vegan if served without dairy

250g (9oz/heaped 1 cup) black beans, soaked in plenty of cold water overnight
2 whole sweet dried chillies, such as New Mexico
2 small hot dried chillies, such as arbol or cascabel
3 whole rich, fruity dried chillies, such as ancho, mulato or pasilla
3 chipotle chillies in adobo or 1 tsp chipotle chilli paste
1.1 litres (37fl oz/generous 4 cups) vegetable stock
400g (14oz) tin of borlotti beans, drained
2 tbsp olive oil
1 large onion, finely chopped
5 tsp cumin seeds
3 garlic cloves, crushed
2 tsp dried oregano
1 tbsp miso paste
1 tsp Marmite or Vegemite
2 × 400g (14oz) tins of plum tomatoes
2 tbsp bourbon
20g (¾oz) dark chocolate (minimum 70% cocoa solids), finely chopped
2 tbsp fine polenta
sea salt and freshly ground black pepper

Drain the soaked black beans, rinse well in a colander and cover with plenty of fresh water in a large saucepan. Bring to the boil and simmer for about 50 minutes until just soft (this will depend on the age of your beans so it could take a little longer). Drain well.

Remove the stalks and seeds from all the dried chilli varieties and put them (whole) in a large, dry flameproof casserole dish (Dutch oven). Place over a medium heat and turn the chillies frequently with tongs for about 3–4 minutes until fragrant and toasted but not burnt. Transfer to a blender with the chillies in adobo and 600ml (20fl oz/2½ cups) of the vegetable stock. Blend until completely smooth, then transfer to a jug, adding the remaining 500ml (17fl oz/2 cups) of stock. Tip the borlotti beans into a bowl, crush with a fork and add to the chilli liquid. It may seem a strange step, but they will add texture to the chilli later.

Return the large casserole to a medium heat and add the olive oil, onion, cumin seeds and a pinch of salt. Cook, stirring, for about 6 minutes until soft and translucent, turning the heat down if needed to prevent them from browning. Add the garlic and oregano and cook for a further minute.

Now add the blitzed chilli and borlotti liquid, miso and Marmite and cook down, stirring, for a further 1–2 minutes to heat through. Stir in the plum tomatoes, followed by the drained black beans. Bring to the boil, then turn down the heat, partially cover and simmer gently for a good 1 hour 30 minutes, or until the black beans are very soft but still just about holding their shape. Stir often to prevent the chilli catching on the base of the pan, turning the heat down and/or adding a dash of water if it keeps doing so. The simmered chilli will still be a little more liquid than is intended.

To serve
cooked quinoa, coriander (cilantro) sprigs, sour cream, avocado and tomatoes dressed with olive oil, Chimichurri (page 169) and lime wedges to squeeze over

Add the bourbon and stir in the chocolate until completely melted. Season to taste with salt (you can adjust again later) and stir in the polenta. Simmer for a few minutes, stirring, to cook out the raw polenta taste and thicken the chilli liquid.

Ideally, you'd let the chilli cool at this point and keep it covered in the fridge for a day or so before reheating thoroughly; the flavours will develop and deepen so much. Taste again when it's cold and has had time to sit, adding a little more salt if needed.

Serve the thoroughly reheated chilli as you like. I have suggested you eat it with cooked quinoa, coriander sprigs, sour cream, avocado and tomatoes dressed with olive oil, chimichurri and lime wedges to squeeze over.

FRESH TOMATO, ROAST PEPPER, CHILLI & BASIL PASTA

A celebratory pasta to make in late summer when tomatoes are bright and ripe. You can make the silky roast pepper and chilli sauce a day or so ahead, ready to toss through hot pasta, fresh tomatoes and a clutch of basil. Serve with a rocket (arugula) salad. A smother of vegetarian hard cheese to finish is optional; there is plenty of flavour here without it.

Serves 4
Preparation time: 20 minutes
Cooking time: 45 minutes
Vegan when eaten without the cheese

100ml (3½fl oz/scant ½ cup) fruity extra virgin olive oil, plus extra to drizzle
6 red Romano peppers, halved
2 large garlic cloves, roughly chopped
1 large red chilli, roughly chopped
2 tbsp sundried tomato purée (paste)
a generous handful of basil leaves, chopped (makes about 2 tbsp), plus extra to garnish
1½ tbsp red wine vinegar
350g (12oz) dried bucatini or other spaghetti-style pasta
300g (10½oz) ripe, flavourful tomatoes, roughly chopped or halved according to size
sea salt and freshly ground black pepper
Pecorino or vegetarian cheese, grated, to serve (optional)

Preheat the oven to 180°C fan (200°C/400°F/gas 6). Brush a roasting tin with a drizzle of oil, spread the peppers, cut-sides down, in the pan in a single layer and roast until they are soft, charred and blistered. This will take about 30 minutes for the thin-skinned, pointed peppers, a little more if you use standard sweet peppers with their more generous padding. Tip into a bowl, cover, then set aside to steam until cool enough to handle. Peel the peppers, discarding the peel, but keeping any collected cooking juices in the bowl.

Put the garlic, chilli and olive oil in a cold frying pan (skillet) and set over a low heat. Cook very gently for 6–7 minutes, adjusting the heat accordingly, so that the garlic is sizzling throughout but barely coloured by the end of the cooking time. Add the tomato purée and cook for a further minute or so, then remove from the heat.

Tip the flavoured oil (with the aromatics) into a blender with 8 of the peeled roast pepper halves and all their juices. Blitz until smooth, then add the chopped basil, red wine vinegar and salt and pepper to taste. Slice the remaining 4 roast pepper halves quite finely and set aside.

Cook the pasta according to the pack instructions until al dente. Drain in a colander, reserving a small cupful of cooking water as you do so. Return the pasta to the saucepan with the pepper sauce and a few tablespoons of pasta cooking water – just enough to make the sauce shiny and cling to the pasta evenly when tossed through in the pan.

Remove from the heat and muddle through the fresh tomatoes, sliced roast peppers and an extra handful of basil leaves. Serve with a drizzle of good oil and yet more basil leaves. This is more than characterful enough eaten as a vegan pasta but can be cloaked with grated Pecorino or vegetarian cheese.

AUBERGINE, BASIL & SWEET POTATO PARMIGIANA

Sacrilege perhaps, to add layers of caramelised sweet potato to the hallowed parmigiana, but they ground this elegant version of the gratin, balancing out the lightest of tomato sauces. I no longer bother salting standard aubergines, to remove excess water, finding it unnecessary for our modern, dense varieties. Dusting the slices with flour and frying, however, proved essential to this recipe; attempts to roast them for simplicity only produced a pappy texture. Work in batches, dusting lightly, then immediately adding them to the hot pan so the flour coating doesn't have time to get soggy. Once fried, the flour creates a golden barrier around each aubergine slice so that they sit in distinct layers.

Serves 4 with salad
Preparation time: 20 minutes
Cooking time: 1 hour 20 minutes

1kg (2lb 4oz) flavourful plum tomatoes, preferably San Marzano
2 large garlic cloves, crushed
about 120ml (4fl oz/½ cup) extra virgin olive oil
550g (1lb 4oz) sweet potatoes, scrubbed and sliced 1cm (½in) thick lengthways
5 oregano sprigs, leaves stripped and chopped
30g (1oz/¼ cup) plain (all-purpose) flour
2 large aubergines (eggplants), sliced a scant 1cm (½in) thick, lengthways
2 tbsp Summer Herb & Seed Pesto (page 175) or ready-made fresh pesto
a large bunch of basil leaves, torn, reserving a few leaves to garnish
250g (9oz) mozzarella, drained and torn into bite-sized pieces
125g (4oz) Parmesan, finely grated
sea salt and freshly ground black pepper
rocket (arugula) or watercress salad, to serve

Skin the tomatoes. Make a shallow cross in the base of each with a knife and place in a large, heatproof bowl. Boil a kettle and pour the boiling water over to cover generously. Leave for 1 minute, then fish out a tomato with a slotted spoon and check if the skin is peeling and pulling away easily from the base. If not, return to the bowl and leave for another minute before draining. The trick is to catch them before the flesh starts to soften, meaning just the fragile skins peel off without taking a layer of flavour with them. Chop roughly, transferring the tomatoes and juice to a medium saucepan as you go. I don't deseed, finding it removes character and flavour.

Add the crushed garlic and a slosh (around 2 tablespoons) of oil to the saucepan. Place over a low heat and bring up to a gentle simmer. Season lightly and cook down for 15 minutes, stirring until the tomatoes are sauce-y, but still retain some texture.

Preheat the oven to 170°C fan (190°C/375°F/gas 5).

Toss the sweet potato slices with 2 tablespoons of oil and the oregano. Season with salt and pepper, spread out on a baking sheet, or sheets, large enough to hold them in a single layer and roast for 20 minutes until just soft and turning golden.

Sift half the flour onto a large plate and season generously with salt and pepper. Place a large frying pan (skillet) over a medium heat and add 1 tablespoon of oil. Working with 4 or 5 aubergine slices at a time (you should have around 14 in total), dredge each one in seasoned flour and dust off the excess. Immediately add to the frying pan and cook for about 2–3 minutes on each side, turning with tongs and reducing the heat if they catch too fast. You want them to just cook through as well as colour. Remove to a clean plate and continue with the remaining slices, refreshing the dredging plate with seasoned, sifted flour halfway through. You'll have a little excess flour left over at the end.

Lightly oil a medium gratin dish – about 20 × 30cm (8 × 12in) or 26cm (10½in) diameter are ideal sizes. Layer up the parmigiana, starting with one-third of the tomato sauce, followed by half the aubergines, half the pesto – spread as best you can – half the sweet potato, half the torn basil leaves, one-third of the mozzarella and one-third of the Parmesan. Repeat the layers once more through, finish with the remaining thirds of tomato sauce, mozzarella and Parmesan. Bake in the middle of the oven (still at the same temperature) for about 50 minutes until deeply golden and bubbling. Leave to rest for 15 minutes to allow the layers to settle and cut cleanly. Adorn with extra basil and serve with a rocket or watercress salad.

BAKED STUFFED TOMATOES
WITH SAFFRON, FENNEL & LENTIL RICE

There was certainly a place for a stuffed tomato in a book of vegetarian bests and ultimates. This variation features sweet fennel and mellow accents of saffron. Seek out large heirloom or beefsteak tomato varieties; they don't have to match, but all eight should weigh around 2.5kg (5lb 10oz) raw. It's a beautiful and good-tempered way to make use of autumnal tomato gluts. With this in mind, you could certainly make it a day ahead, chill overnight and serve at room temperature the following day.

Serves 8
Preparation time: 30 minutes
Cooking time: 1 hour 30 minutes

a pinch of saffron stamens
1 tbsp olive oil
3 shallots, chopped
1 medium fennel bulb, trimmed and
    finely chopped
3 garlic cloves, crushed
1 tbsp tomato purée (paste)
250g (9oz/heaped 1 cup) risotto rice
1 small glass of dry white wine
500ml (17fl oz/2 cups) vegetable stock
60g (2oz) Parmesan, finely grated
    (optional)
8 large heirloom or beefsteak tomatoes
    (total weight about 2.5kg (5lb 10oz))
225g (8oz/heaped 1 cup) cooked and
    drained green lentils
6 sundried tomatoes, drained
    and chopped
4 oregano sprigs, leaves stripped
    and chopped
4 thyme sprigs, leaves stripped
    and chopped
a handful of dill fronds, finely
    chopped
a handful of basil leaves,
    finely chopped
a handful of flat-leaf parsley leaves,
    finely chopped
a drizzle of extra virgin olive oil
sea salt and freshly ground black
    pepper
4 tbsp Saffron & Paprika Rouille
    (page 173), to serve (optional)
a leafy green salad, to serve

Start by making the rice filling, which is essentially a 'lazy' risotto. Pour 2 tablespoons of just-boiled water over the saffron stamens in a small cup and set aside to steep.

Put the tablespoon of oil in a medium saucepan and set over a lowish heat. Add the shallots and fennel with a good pinch of salt and sizzle gently, stirring often, for 7–8 minutes until softened but not coloured. Stir in the garlic and tomato purée and cook for barely a minute, then add the rice and stir to coat. Turn the heat up a touch, slosh the wine in (you don't have to, but it adds flavour) and simmer until almost evaporated. Now add 400ml (13fl oz/generous 1½ cups) of stock and simmer briskly for 15–16 minutes, adding the remaining stock after 12 minutes if needed. Stir the mixture often, especially towards the end of the cooking time as it could easily catch as it thickens. By the end, the rice should be somewhere near cooked, but still chalky in texture, and the liquid almost gone. Remove from the heat and stir in the Parmesan, if using, and the steeped saffron mixture. Set aside to cool a little.

Preheat the oven to 150°C fan (170°C/340°F/gas 3).

Place the tomatoes on a chopping board with an empty bowl alongside. Ideally using a serrated knife, cut the tops off the tomatoes horizontally. Scoop the exposed insides out with a spoon – such large tomatoes tend to have quite dense innards – and hold each one over the bowl to scrape the remaining seeds away. Roughly dice the scooped-out flesh, discarding any tough cores.

Stir this diced tomato flesh into the rice with the lentils, sundried tomatoes and herbs. Add black pepper and a little salt to taste; it should be quite highly seasoned. It's fine to taste-check the mixture, even though the rice will be a little under. Drizzle a large baking dish or tin with a little oil, then add the hollowed-out tomatoes. Spoon the rice filling into them generously (but don't pack it in too tightly or the tomatoes will split). Replace the lids and drizzle with a little more oil.

Bake the tomatoes for 1 hour until completely tender, but still holding their shape, buffered by jellied olive oil juices. Serve them warm or at room temperature, perhaps with spoonfuls of saffron and paprika rouille and definitely with a leafy salad.

WHOLEGRAIN NASI GORENG

Indonesia's egg fried rice, *nasi goreng,* will comfort like no other dish. This is a love letter to its resonant flavours and the fresh, quirky finishing touches that make and balance the dish.

The depth of flavour comes from a fresh chilli paste, fried off before the rice. I use salty, umami-rich miso in place of the traditional shrimp paste – it works wonderfully – and the essential sweet *kecap manis* (readily available in supermarkets). The labour here is in the chopping and prepping; the fried rice itself will come together in minutes. You'll need cooked and chilled wholegrain or brown rice – long or short grain will work fine – and you can use packs of ready-cooked rice instead of cooking and chilling dried rice from scratch.

Serves 4
Preparation time: 40 minutes
Cooking time: 10 minutes

For the miso-chilli paste
4 shallots, roughly chopped
2 garlic cloves, roughly chopped
1 tbsp miso paste (any you have)
2 tsp sundried tomato purée (paste)
2 large red chillies, chopped
2 tbsp groundnut (peanut) oil

For the nasi goreng
about 4 tbsp groundnut (peanut) oil
150g (5oz) shiitake mushrooms, sliced
150g (5oz) green beans, trimmed and
    cut into 4cm (2½in) pieces
5 garlic cloves, sliced
7 medium eggs, 3 lightly beaten
380g (13oz/2¾ cups) cooked and
    chilled rice (this is about 150g
    (5oz/heaped ¾ cup) uncooked)
1 tbsp light soy sauce
2 tbsp *kecap manis*
1–2 red chillies, sliced (birdseye, if liked)
5 spring onions (scallions), trimmed
    and finely sliced
sea salt and freshly ground black pepper

**To finish, choose all or any of
the following**
a handful of tomatoes, halved or
    quartered, depending on size
½ midi cucumber, cut into chunks
175g (6oz) trimmed fresh pineapple,
    sliced
a handful of coriander (cilantro) sprigs
1–2 birdseye chillies, sliced
2 spring onions (scallions), trimmed
    and finely shredded
2 tbsp crispy fried onions
2 tbsp roasted peanuts
1 lime, sliced into wedges
sriracha chilli sauce or Fragrant Chilli
    Oil (see page 172)

Put all the ingredients for the chilli paste in a small blender or pestle and mortar and whizz or pound until fairly smooth.

Heat 1 tablespoon of the oil in a large wok or deep frying pan (skillet) set over a high heat. Stir-fry the mushrooms and beans hard in this for 2–3 minutes until just beginning to brown. Tip onto a plate and set aside.

To make the nasi goreng, return the pan to the heat with 1½ tablespoons of oil and the garlic, frying until pale golden but not brown. Immediately pour in the 3 beaten eggs. Leave to cook until half-set, then break up with a wooden spoon or spatula. Carry on frying the egg until it's just beginning to brown, then tip in the chilli paste and cook for a minute or so. Remove from the heat while you fry the remaining 4 whole eggs to top the nasi goreng.

To do this, use a separate, large frying pan set over a medium heat. Add 1½ tablespoons of oil and crack in the 4 eggs. Flick the hot oil over the eggs occasionally until they are golden at the edges with barely set whites and runny yolks. This should take 3–4 minutes. Remove from the heat, remembering they will continue to cook through so undershoot it slightly.

Add the cooked rice to the chilli paste pan, returning it to a high heat, and stir-fry until sizzling. You really want the grains to catch and crisp up. Stir in the soy sauce, *kecap manis*, 1–2 sliced chillies (to taste) and the spring onions. Stir to combine and sizzle, then return the cooked mushrooms and beans to the pan.

Fry briskly, stirring, for another minute or so, then taste and season with salt and pepper. Divide among serving plates. Top each with a fried egg straight from the pan and accompany with all the trimmings you chose and prepared. If you've gone for everything, this will be the tomatoes, cucumber, pineapple, coriander, sliced chillies, shredded spring onion tops, fried onions, peanuts, lime wedges and chilli sauce or chilli oil.

IMAM BAYALDI STUFFED AUBERGINES & COURGETTES

Though it has its own humble charm, this recipe couldn't be described as a looker. To compensate, it is more delicious than I can tell you. Please make it. Stuffed, baked vegetables require some work, but most of the magic happens after the leisurely cooking; somehow the flavours get infinitely better after two to four days, deepening and rounding out as the vegetables sit in the fridge. When needed, serve at room temperature or reheat thoroughly in a low oven before scattering with the pistachios, parsley and pomegranates to finish, as below.

Serves 4
Preparation time: 30 minutes, plus cooling
Cooking time: 2 hours 40 minutes
Vegan

150ml (5fl oz/scant ⅔ cup) extra virgin olive oil
4 medium, slender aubergines (eggplants)
4 medium courgettes (zucchini)
2 red onions, finely sliced
1 red (bell) pepper, deseeded and finely sliced
8 garlic cloves, chopped
2 × 400g (14oz) tins of good-quality, finely chopped tomatoes
½ tsp ground cinnamon
1 tsp smoked paprika
1 tsp dried oregano
a small bunch of flat-leaf parsley leaves, finely chopped
a small bunch of basil leaves, chopped
½ small bunch of dill fronds, finely chopped
2 tbsp red wine vinegar
a large pinch of sugar
a large pinch of sea salt
a large pinch of freshly ground black pepper
50g (1¾oz/⅓ cup) shelled pistachios, toasted and chopped
a small handful of flat-leaf parsley leaves, chopped
50g (1¾oz) pomegranate arials
bread, a steamed wholegrain or lentils and a dressed salad of bitter leaves, to serve

Preheat the oven to fan 210°C (230°C/450°F/gas 8). Line a roasting tin with kitchen foil and brush or drizzle sparingly with olive oil.

Cut a deep slit in the aubergines and the courgettes through their middles, being careful not to slice them in half. Place in the pan and bake for 25 minutes until the outer skins begin to shrivel. Remove from the oven and put in a colander in the sink to drain, cut-sides down. Leave for 30 minutes. Keep the (unwashed) roasting tin handy.

While the vegetables bake, put 2 tablespoons of olive oil in a large, deep frying pan (skillet) set over a medium heat. Add the onions and pepper and cook, stirring often, until very soft but not browned. This will take around 15 minutes. Now add the garlic and cook for 30 seconds more. Stir in the tomatoes, cinnamon, paprika and dried oregano. Bring to the boil, then allow to simmer and reduce down for 10 minutes, stirring. Remove from the heat and leave to cool for 15 minutes. Reserve a handful of parsley for garnish, then stir in 90ml (3fl oz/generous ⅓ cup) of olive oil with the chopped herbs, vinegar, sugar, salt and pepper. At this point, both vegetables and sauce can be covered and chilled (separately) for up to 2 days. Bring up to room temperature when ready to continue with the recipe.

When ready to cook, preheat the oven to 150°C fan (170°C/340°F/gas 3).

Put the drained whole courgettes and aubergines back in their roasting tin, slit-sides up. Gently prise the vegetables open, being careful not to split their skins any further. Spoon the tomato mixture into the openings as neatly as possible. It doesn't matter if some overflows and drops down into the pan. Drizzle the vegetables with the remaining olive oil and pour 3 tablespoons of hot water into the base of the tin. Season and cover tightly with kitchen foil, sealing the edges well.

Bake in the middle of the oven for 1 hour 40 minutes or so until they are almost falling apart. The juices in the bottom of the pan should be caramelised and greatly reduced. Leave to cool for 20 minutes, then scatter with the pistachios, parsley and pomegranate arials to serve.

Eat with excellent bread, a steamed wholegrain or lentils and a dressed salad of bitter leaves. Non-vegan additions include crumbled feta or spoonfuls of tzatziki, if dairy is welcome.

THE GAZPACHO

I've put this iconic Spanish-inspired chilled soup in the Supper chapter because it's got every trimming going. Far too much, I thought, to call it a small plate, though I suppose you may wish to serve this as a starter anyway. I'd call gazpacho a main on a hot day or balmy evening, perhaps adding a leafy lentil salad with bread alongside or beforehand. Gazpacho flavours need to be bright and clean, so you'll find plenty of tomatoes here, plus the sting of vinegar, but a little less in the way of bread and blended-in oil. The number of garnishes applied is up to you, but they're what make this soup so special; I'd recommend ticking off as many as possible. The list – not always strictly Spanish – can include chopped olives, capers and chillies, summer herbs, a herb pistou or oil, chopped fresh tomatoes and cucumber, chopped raw or roast peppers, chopped hard-boiled egg, diced shallot and, a must I feel, a toasted herb-flecked breadcrumb.

Serves 4 generously
Preparation time: 25 minutes,
plus chilling
Cooking time: 15 minutes, depending
on the topping choices

For the gazpacho
75g (2½oz) stale white sourdough bread
1.2kg (2lb 6oz) very ripe tomatoes,
　roughly diced
2 ripe red (bell) peppers, deseeded
　and diced
1 medium cucumber, peeled, deseeded
　and diced
2 garlic cloves, roughly chopped
2 tbsp best-quality sundried tomato
　purée (paste)
150ml (5fl oz/scant ⅔ cup) extra virgin
　olive oil, plus a little extra to serve
2 tbsp good sherry vinegar or red
　wine vinegar

For the herb crumb
75g (2½oz) stale sourdough bread,
　torn into bite-sized pieces
2 tbsp Summer Herb & Seed Pesto
　(page 175) or other pesto
1 tbsp olive oil
sea salt and freshly ground black pepper

For the toppings
2 eggs, hard-boiled and chopped
2 shallots, finely chopped
8 black or green olives, stoned
　and chopped
1 tbsp capers, rinsed and drained
¼ cucumber, finely diced
½ red, yellow or green (bell) pepper,
　deseeded and finely diced
1 mild red chilli, sliced
2 basil, mint or parsley sprigs,
　leaves stripped

Prepare the toppings of your choice, selecting some or all, and set aside or chill until needed. If you wish to include the hard-boiled eggs, cook them up to a few hours in advance by covering with cold water in a small saucepan. Bring to the boil over a medium heat and simmer gently for 7 minutes. Drain, refresh under cold water, then peel and chill the eggs, dicing when needed.

If you wish to include the toasted herb breadcrumbs as a topping – and I recommend you do – put the torn sourdough in a mini food processor or a blender with the pesto and blitz to breadcrumbs. Season with salt and pepper. Put the oil in a frying pan (skillet) set over a medium heat and add the pesto crumbs. Now cook, stirring near-constantly, for 5–6 minutes until evenly golden and crisp. Leave to cool and store in an airtight container for up to 3 days.

To make the soup, put the bread in a shallow bowl, cover with cold water and leave to soak for 20 minutes. Put the tomatoes and peppers in a blender or food processor with the cucumber and garlic. Squeeze out the bread and tear that in. Finish with the 150ml (5fl oz/scant ⅔ cup) olive oil, blending until completely smooth.

Pass the soup through a sieve, pushing and scraping with a spatula to force all the liquid through. Discard the dry solids left in the sieve, then stir the vinegar into the soup and season to taste with salt. Remember it will be served well chilled so the seasoning will need to be a little stronger than usual. Cover and refrigerate for at least 4 hours or overnight until thoroughly chilled. The flavours will deepen and settle as it chills through so aim to make this a day ahead of time, if possible.

Top each generous serving of chilled soup with a selection of the toppings suggested. You can add them yourself or serve them on the table, letting your guests add their own choices to taste.

SIDES

Never to be side-lined, these are the good bits and an equally important chapter as The Sauce.

You won't find any plain steamed greens here; you already know how to gussy those up with flavoured butters or dressings – and if you are short on ideas, just head to The Sauce chapter for inspiration. I want to add real value to your modern repertoire of side dishes, so I've honed in on character, texture and blasts of flavour, not to mention the nutritional benefits of adding more seasonal vegetables to your table, with all the valuable fibre and micronutrients they bring.

This is a chapter with widespread appeal as the recipes are particularly lively, making them versatile to stand alone or work as impactful accompaniments on any table, vegetarian or not.

Many of these clever ideas can be combined to make a meal. For example, the Roast Harissa Roots are superb with the Kale Salad or the Greek-Inspired Baked Butter Beans. Mix and match as you wish. Accompanied by, say, lovely cheeses, breads, salad leaves or grains, make one of these sides the star of your table and not an also-ran. In fact, I have written them with this in mind and have recommended ways to build a whole meal from each one. If you're taken with making a side recipe alone as a highly flavoured main course – and there are no rules to say that you shouldn't – I would recommend assuming a recipe designated to serve four will feed two as a main meal.

However you choose to serve them, sassy sides are the way ahead.

LEMON SPRING GREENS

Not spring greens with lemon, as it were, but the most vibrant and delicate spring vegetables doused with a warm lemon, herb and mustard vinaigrette. You can use melted butter here instead of the olive oil for a non-vegan variation. If you don't fancy preparing fresh artichokes from scratch, you can miss out that step entirely, using marinated artichoke hearts. Drain them of their marinade, halve or slice as you prefer and add them to the other vegetables towards the end of their steaming time to warm through.

Serves 4–6 as a side
Preparation time: 30 minutes
Cooking time: 10 minutes
Vegan

4 young globe artichokes
finely grated zest and juice of 1 lemon
300g (10½oz) podded broad (fava)
    beans
6 fine spring onions (scallions),
    trimmed, and cut into 4cm
    (2½in) lengths
a small bunch of fine asparagus,
    trimmed
200g (7oz) podded peas
150g (5oz) fine green beans
4 tbsp extra virgin olive oil
2 tbsp white wine vinegar
4 tbsp finely chopped mixed summer
    herb leaves such as chervil, dill,
    chives, mint, basil, plus a few extra
    sprigs or leaves to garnish
1 heaped tsp wholegrain mustard
a pinch of unrefined caster
    (superfine) sugar

Trim each artichoke brutally, slicing and paring the tough outer leaves away, trimming any excess stalk down to a few centimetres in length and lopping off the top of each so that the leaves are trimmed straight and the hairy central choke is revealed. Remove these chokes with a sturdy teaspoon, hoiking everything out to leave just the hearts, tender trimmed leaves and short stalks behind. Halve or quarter the hearts if large. As each one is finished, immediately transfer to a bowl of water with the juice of ½ lemon to stop them turning brown.

Put the podded broad beans in a bowl and pour boiling water from the kettle over to just cover. Set aside for 8–10 minutes, then tip into a colander and slip the outer skin from the beans to reveal their emerald-green innards.

Drain the prepared artichoke hearts and put them in a steamer fitted over a pan of simmering water and steam for 3 minutes. Add the spring onions, asparagus, peas and green beans and steam for a further 4 minutes until just tender.

Combine the remaining lemon juice with the grated zest, the olive oil, vinegar, chopped herbs, mustard and pinch of sugar. It's easiest to do this in a lidded jar, shaking it vigorously to combine, but you could use a small whisk and a bowl.

When the vegetables are just tender, drain and add to the drained-out water pan below the steamer with the double-podded broad beans and the dressing. Warm through over a gentle heat for 1–2 minutes before serving with a few fresh herb sprigs or leaves for garnish.

ROAST AUBERGINE WITH SESAME & SPRING ONION

Elegant aubergine (eggplant) wedges are slowly roasted until golden and silky-soft, then dressed with sesame oil, ponzu sauce, toasted sesame seeds and shredded spring onions (scallions). If you can't buy ponzu sauce – which often contains yuzu juice, a tart mixture of lime juice, lemon juice, honey or maple syrup – mirin and soy will do as a substitute. Make this into supper by accompanying with steamed brown or red rice and crisp-edged tofu or a chilli omelette.

Serves 4 as a side
Preparation time: 20 minutes
Cooking time: 45 minutes
Vegan if made without honey

3 smallish aubergines (eggplants), trimmed and sliced into 6 wedges
2 tbsp groundnut (peanut) or other neutral oil
1½ tbsp sesame seeds
4 spring onions (scallions), white parts sliced and green parts finely shredded
a thumb of ginger root, peeled and finely shredded
2 garlic cloves, sliced
1 red or green chilli, finely sliced
2 tbsp toasted sesame oil
2 tbsp ponzu (sauce)
2 tsp honey or maple syrup
2 tbsp light soy sauce
2 tbsp lime juice
a small handful of Thai basil leaves
sea salt and freshly ground black pepper
lime wedges, to squeeze over (optional)

Preheat the oven to 170°C fan (190°C/375°F/gas 5).

Toss the aubergine with 1½ tablespoons of groundnut oil and spread out in a roasting tin in a single layer, making sure the base of the tin is well-greased with oil. Season with salt and pepper and roast for 40 minutes, or until the wedges are golden and very soft but still holding their shape.

Toast the sesame seeds in a dry frying pan (skillet) set over a medium heat for 2–3 minutes. Shake the pan often until the seeds are an even and pale shade of gold.

Put the remaining ½ tablespoon of groundnut oil in a frying pan and add the sliced whiter parts of the spring onion with the ginger, garlic and chilli. Place over a medium heat and, once the aromatics begin to gently sizzle, stir-fry for around 6 minutes until just golden and frazzled in appearance. Transfer to a bowl.

Combine the sesame oil, ponzu, honey or syrup, soy sauce and lime juice. Spoon over the aubergines, followed by the frazzled aromatic mixture, the shredded fresh spring onion greens, toasted sesame seeds and Thai basil leaves. Offer extra lime wedges to squeeze over, if you like.

TWICE-ROAST BEETROOT IN A FIG & WATERCRESS SALAD

These slightly chewy, candy-sweet wedges of beetroot are first baked whole in kitchen foil, then cut into wedges and slowly roasted to concentrate and caramelise. I have taken this a step further and suggested a jaunty salad of figs, watercress, goats' cheese and Chimichurri to showcase them. You could swap in any herb vinaigrette for the chimichurri or ignore the latter part of the recipe completely, simply adding the twice-roast beets to a cheeseboard, piling onto chargrilled toast spread thickly with soft cheese and herbs, or scattering into a lentil salad.

Serves 4 as a side or a salad
Preparation time: 30 minutes
Cooking time: 2 hours 15 minutes

For the twice-roast beetroots
4 medium beetroots (beets),
     stalks trimmed
2 tbsp olive oil
½ tsp fennel seeds, crushed
extra virgin olive oil, to drizzle
1 tbsp red wine vinegar

For the salad
2 large handfuls of watercress sprigs,
     tough stalks removed
4–5 tbsp Chimichurri (page 169)
extra virgin olive oil, to drizzle
3 ripe figs, torn into pieces
50g (1¾oz/½ cup) toasted walnuts,
     roughly crushed
150g (5oz) French soft goats' cheese
sea salt and freshly ground
     black pepper

Preheat the oven to 180°C fan (200°C/400°F/gas 6).

Scrub the beetroots to remove any dirt but leave the water clinging to them. Enclose each wet beetroot in a square of kitchen foil. Place the parcels on a baking sheet and roast for about 1 hour until tender when a skewer is inserted into the middle. Timings will, of course, depend on their size. Leave until cool enough to handle, then cut into bite-sized wedges, peeling first with a sharp knife if the skins appear tough.

Now turn the oven to 130°C fan (150°C/300°F/gas 2). Coat the beetroot wedges with the olive oil and spread out across a large roasting tin. Season well with salt and pepper and bake for a further 1 hour until the beetroots have turned darker and dehydrated enough to be slightly chewy. Add the crushed fennel seeds and cook for a further 15 minutes. Remove from the oven and toss with a generous tablespoon of extra virgin olive oil and the red wine vinegar to glaze in the pan. Leave to cool. The beets will keep, covered, in the fridge for up to 5 days.

To make the salad, toss the dressed beetroots through the watercress sprigs in a bowl with 2–3 tablespoons of chimichurri dressing and a glug of extra virgin olive oil. Gently tumble in the torn figs and toasted walnuts, seasoning lightly with salt and pepper. Divide between serving plates, tucking in the goats' cheese and drizzling with a touch more chimichurri and extra virgin olive oil.

SHIITAKE SKEWERS

A vegan barbecue side with style. Do use a barbecue to cook these instead of the griddle pan suggested, if you can. The quantities are easily doubled to serve more, but you can make this into a simple lunch or light supper as shown in the image by adding some sprightly greens and a mixture of tender wholegrain rice varieties. In that case, you'll need two skewers per person and should perhaps go easier on the teriyaki-style marinade, which is designed to be rich and syrupy to pack a real flavour punch.

**Makes 4 skewers, serves 4 as a side
or 2 as a main**
Preparation time: 20 minutes
Cooking time: 10 minutes
Vegan

6 spring onions (scallions), trimmed
    and cut into 4cm (2½in) lengths
200g (7oz) (about 16) shiitake
    mushrooms, halved if large
1 tbsp toasted sesame oil
2 tsp toasted sesame seeds

For the teriyaki marinade
a small thumb of ginger root, peeled
    and finely grated
1 large garlic clove, crushed
2 tbsp light soft brown sugar
3 tbsp mirin
3 tbsp light soy sauce
2 tbsp rice wine vinegar
1½ tbsp toasted sesame oil

To make a teriyaki-style marinade for the skewers, put the ginger, garlic, sugar, mirin and soy sauce in a small saucepan. Set over a medium heat and bring to the boil. Simmer very gently for 2–3 minutes until slightly syrupy. Remove from the heat and stir in the rice wine vinegar and toasted sesame oil. Leave to cool or keep warm in the pan if you're using straight away.

If you don't have metal skewers, soak wooden ones in plenty of cool water for at least 15 minutes, then drain. This will prevent them scorching.

Thread lengths of spring onion onto the skewers, snugly interspersed with the shiitake mushrooms. You should be able to fit about 4 whole mushrooms onto each skewer with the spring onions stacked in between. Brush lightly with the toasted sesame oil.

Place a griddle pan over a high heat and allow to come up to temperature. Place the marinade back over the heat and have a heatproof brush ready. Griddle the skewers for a minute or so on each side, brushing generously with the marinade every time you turn them, cooking for around 5 minutes in total until charred in places, glazed and cooked through. Scatter with sesame seeds and serve as a barbecue side.

Alternatively, serve two skewers per person as a light supper over a steamed wholegrain rice mix with salad leaves, snipped sprouts and shredded spring onion tops. Drizzle any remaining marinade over to finish.

KALE SALAD

Doubtless worthy of the vegetarian classic title, here is the ultimate umami and texture-rich kale salad. It's here in Sides but is also a lunch or supper in itself (serving two). Use a robust kale of any kind; curly types in green or purple colourways or cavolo nero, also known as Tuscan kale, in any combination are ideal.

Serves 4 as a side
Preparation time: 25 minutes
Cooking time: 10 minutes

300g (10½oz) robust kale, central
    stalks removed and leaves torn
    into bite-sized pieces
4 tbsp extra virgin olive oil
50g (1¾oz/⅓ cup) pumpkin seeds
50g (1¾oz) mature Pecorino
½ tsp dried chilli (hot pepper) flakes
1 large garlic clove, crushed
1 tsp Dijon mustard
finely grated zest and juice of 1 lemon
2 tsp maple syrup or honey
1 small pomegranate, arials removed
    (120g (40z) weight of arials only)
30g (1oz/scant ¼ cup) smoked
    almonds, roughly chopped
sea salt and freshly ground
    black pepper

Preheat the oven to 180°C fan (200°C/400°F/gas 6).

Put the kale pieces in a large bowl and, using clean hands, 'massage' 1 tablespoon of olive oil into them to coat thoroughly, bruising them in the process. Set aside for 15 minutes.

Spread the pumpkin seeds out on an oiled baking sheet in a single layer. Finely grate 25g (1oz) of the Pecorino over the seeds and scatter the chilli flakes over that. Season with black pepper and bake for 6–8 minutes until the cheese and seeds are golden and beginning to crisp up. Leave to cool, then break into pieces.

To make the dressing, shake the remaining olive oil, the garlic, mustard, lemon zest and juice, maple syrup or honey, 1 tablespoon of water and salt and pepper together to taste to make a thick dressing. Adjust the sweetness, lemon or mustard, as you prefer, to make a sharp, strong dressing.

Combine the dressing with the massaged kale, tossing to coat thoroughly. Shave in the remaining Pecorino using a vegetable peeler, then gently toss through with the pomegranate arials, smoked almonds and pumpkin-pecorino shards.

SMOKY ROAST CAULIFLOWER
WITH CAPERS & LEMON

A side designed to be the base of a meal. This roast cauliflower is sweet and mellow, balanced by the piquancy of lemon flesh, parsley and capers. We haven't shown it in the photograph as the whole cauliflower was so handsome, but the Basil & Lemon Pistou makes an ideal accompaniment to keep the table vegan and add another layer of vibrancy. Otherwise, one of the mayonnaise-style sauces from The Sauce, the Piri Piri Everything (page 176) or any kind of pesto would be very fine with this, plus, as mentioned in the method below, dressed lentils or a bitter leaf salad.

Serves 4–6 with other sides
Preparation time: 25 minutes
Cooking time: 1 hour 35 minutes
Vegan

1 extra-large (1.5kg/3lb 5oz)
    cauliflower, tough or excess
    outer leaves removed and base
    trimmed flat
2 tsp sweet smoked paprika
2 tsp cumin seeds
6 tbsp extra virgin olive oil, plus
    extra to taste
2 garlic cloves, crushed
2 tbsp maple syrup
3 tbsp sherry vinegar
2 tsp finely chopped thyme leaves
2 lemons, finely grated zest and
    reserve the lemons
2 tbsp tiny capers, rinsed and drained
2 tbsp roughly chopped flat-leaf
    parsley leaves
sea salt and freshly ground
    black pepper
Basil & Lemon Pistou (page 180),
    to serve
chicory or rocket (arugula) salad or
    mustard-dressed lentils, to serve

Steam the whole cauliflower in a lidded steamer or colander set over simmering water for 20 minutes. Drain and leave to cool for a few minutes until the cauliflower is cool enough to handle.

Meanwhile, preheat the oven to 170°C fan (190°C/375°F/gas 5).

Combine the paprika and cumin seeds with 2 tablespoons of the olive oil in a bowl. Season this mixture well with salt and pepper, then rub it over the surface of the cauliflower. Set it in a large casserole (Dutch oven), cover with the lid and roast for about 1 hour, or until tender in the middle when a skewer is poked in.

In a small bowl, combine the garlic with the maple syrup, sherry vinegar, thyme and 1 tablespoon of olive oil. Season well with salt and pepper and set aside.

Top and tail one of the zested lemons, revealing the flesh at either end. Slice the peel and white pith away, following the shape of the fruit to leave the flesh intact. Slice between the membranes to remove the lemon segments. Roughly chop these. Combine this chopped lemon flesh with the remaining olive oil, capers, all the lemon zest, the juice of the remaining lemon and the parsley.

Remove the lid from the cauliflower, spoon over the garlic dressing and continue to roast for 10 minutes until golden. Either keep the cauliflower in the pot and take straight to the table or carefully transfer to a serving platter and spoon the caper mixture over. Serve with the pistou on the side. A crisp chicory or rocket salad and perhaps some mustard-dressed lentils go well.

SMASHED POTATOES WITH OLIVES & SAGE

This is a straightforward recipe, but it needs nothing more. Just a handful of olives pack a real punch when roasted; their salt and savoury notes become concentrated and pair perfectly with crisp-edged, smashed potatoes. Serve with salad and the vegan-friendly Basil & Lemon Pistou (page 180). Or, to go in a non-vegan direction, throw some crumbled blue cheese into a salad and accompany the spuds with Tarragon & Cornichon Aioli (page 176) or Herb Mayonnaise (page 180).

Serves 6 as a side
Preparation time: 15 minutes
Cooking time: 1 hour
Vegan

1kg (2lb 4 oz) small, waxy new
    potatoes, halved if on the larger side
4 tbsp extra virgin olive oil
150g (5oz) black and green olives,
    stoned and halved if large
6 garlic cloves, left whole in skins
a handful of sage leaves
sea salt and freshly ground
    black pepper

Preheat the oven to 180°C fan (200°C/400°F/gas 6).

Bring a large pan of lightly salted water to the boil and parboil the potatoes for 10 minutes. Drain in a colander.

Tip the drained potatoes into a large roasting tin and, using the base of a mug or bowl, gently crush to flatten slightly. Drizzle with the oil and season lightly with salt. Roast for 25 minutes.

Scatter the olives, garlic and sage over the potatoes, shimmying the pan to combine evenly and shuffle the potatoes about a bit. Cook for a further 25 minutes, or until crisp and golden. Season with a little more salt and lots of black pepper.

MUSTARD-DRESSED PULSES WITH HERBS

The perfect sharp and sweet Grain Mustard Vinaigrette melts and absorbs into warm pulses – a mix of green and Puy lentils, for example – to dress and elevate. Throw in sweet sliced shallots and plenty of soft summer herbs – such as chervil, mint, basil, parsley and dill – with more judicious amounts of tarragon, oregano or marjoram. Eat as a summery side for barbecues or picnics. Peppery salad leaves and shaved fennel or sliced heirloom tomatoes will stretch the pulses further but may need a slick of great olive oil, depending on how many you add. As the seasons change, turn the lentil, bean or chickpea base into an autumnal main course salad with cubes of roast pumpkin or beetroot, Baked Red Onion Petals (page 156), toasted seeds and a salty cheese such as crumbled feta or Roquefort.

To get the required quantity of cooked lentils, you need about 300g (10½oz/1⅔ cups) dried lentils, so simmer from scratch, bearing in mind that different varieties will cook to tenderness at different times, or use ready-cooked beans or lentils, warming them through before draining and proceeding with the recipe.

Serves 6 as a side
Preparation time: 20 minutes
Vegan

8 tbsp Grain Mustard Vinaigrette
    (page 175)
2 large banana shallots (echalions),
    finely sliced
600g (1lb 5oz/3 cups) warm, cooked
    Puy lentils or other pulses, drained
2 handfuls of summer herbs, chopped
    (see intro)
sea salt and freshly ground
    black pepper

Add half the dressing and the sliced shallots to the warm, drained lentils or other pulses. Set aside for 10 minutes, stirring now and then. Add the remaining dressing and the chopped herbs, tumbling through to combine and seasoning to taste. That's it. Vary and build on this stalwart blueprint as you wish.

SLOW-COOKED COURGETTES
WITH SALTED RICOTTA & PINE NUTS.

A tender, jammy mix of braised courgette which makes an excellent pasta sauce or can be stirred into risotto at the end of cooking. To showcase it as a topping for toasted focaccia, I have added salted ricotta, pine nuts, a chilli relish and shavings of raw courgette for texture. If using sourdough instead, toast or griddle slices until slightly charred, then I'd recommend rubbing one side with cut garlic and drizzling with olive oil. On that matter, best-quality olive oil is essential here; choose one with plenty of green, fruit or pepper notes. Ideally you'd be using up a summer glut of green or yellow courgettes, or even patty pan squash.

The Chilli-Pepper Jam is on the less sweet end. If using a similar, ready-made relish or chilli jam, taste for sweetness and consider letting down with a dash of red wine or balsamic vinegar to keep the flavours of this dish balanced; it shouldn't be overly saccharine.

Serves 4
Preparation time: 20 minutes
Cooking time: 1 hour 30 minutes

1.3kg (2lb 13oz) smallish courgettes (zucchini), trimmed
5 tbsp fruity extra virgin olive oil, plus extra to serve
4 large garlic cloves, sliced
1 tsp chopped oregano leaves
2–3 tbsp lemon juice, to taste
2 tbsp pine nuts
400g (14oz) focaccia or 4 large slices of sourdough bread
3 tbsp Chilli-Pepper Jam (page 169) or a ready-made relish
150g (5oz) ricotta salata, sliced or shaved
a small handful of basil leaves
sea salt and freshly ground black pepper

Cut all the courgettes but one half into 5mm (¼in) thick slices, setting the remaining half aside in the fridge for later.

Put 2 tablespoons of the olive oil in a large, lidded flameproof casserole (Dutch oven) or heavy-based saucepan set over a low heat. Stir in the garlic, sliced courgettes and oregano. Season with salt and pepper, partially cover and leave to cook for about 1 hour 20 minutes, stirring now and then. Once ready, the oil should have separated from the very soft and reduced courgette mixture, but there won't be much liquid in the pan. If there is, remove the lid completely and simmer down until nearly all the water has evaporated. Taste and adjust the seasoning with salt and pepper, adding a touch (1–2 tablespoons) of lemon juice to brighten if needed, but remembering the salted ricotta will add extra salt.

Toast the pine nuts with 1 tablespoon of olive oil in a frying pan (skillet) set over a low heat. Stand over the pan, shaking it often, for a couple of minutes until the pine nuts are golden. Drain on paper towels.

Shave the remaining courgette half into ribbons with a vegetable peeler and dress lightly with salt, pepper, olive oil and a few drops of lemon juice.

If using focaccia, halve horizontally and toast under a lowish grill for a few minutes to warm through and crisp a little. Cut into 8 pieces so they're manageable to handle and eat.

Either way, pile the cooked courgettes up on top of the bread, followed by the raw, dressed courgettes in a light pile. Tuck in the chilli relish in spoonfuls with shavings or rough slices of ricotta salata, the toasted pine nuts and basil leaves. Drizzle with more of your best extra virgin olive oil to serve.

ROAST HARISSA ROOTS

I use a rose harissa paste here; you want an oily, fiery, rambunctious one. Cheaper and/or overly sweet pastes will catch and burn too quickly in the oven. Perhaps it's obvious, but by 'rainbow' carrots, I simply mean a selection of yellow, orange, purple, red – whatever is available. The vegetables are easily doubled or varied; add or swap in scrubbed baby beetroot (beets), wedges of squash or slices of sweet potato.

There are endless ways of making this side into something more substantial. Scatter with a citrus-dressed mixture of chopped toasted pistachios, slivered dates, chopped parsley and crumbled feta. Tumble in a tin of drained chickpeas (garbanzos) and a half teaspoon of hot smoked paprika when drizzling with honey towards the end of the cooking time, then shower with Dukkah (page 183), homemade or ready-made. Serve the sticky roots over a mountain of finely chopped parsley and mint, studded with soaked bulgar wheat, lemon juice, olive oil, toasted mixed seeds and pomegranate arials.

Serves 4 as a side
Preparation time: 15 minutes
Cooking time: 50 minutes

8 baby parsnips, scrubbed and
   halved if large
12 slender rainbow carrots
4 shallots, halved or quartered if large
1 lemon, thickly sliced
2 tbsp extra virgin olive oil
2 tbsp oily harissa paste, well-stirred
2 garlic bulbs, halved
2 tsp honey
1½ tsp cumin seeds
sea salt and freshly ground
   black pepper

Preheat the oven to 170°C fan (190°C/375°F/gas 5).

Toss the parsnips, carrots, shallots and lemon slices together with the oil and harissa in a bowl. Season well and spread out in a roasting tin, tucking in the halved garlic bulbs, making sure they get coated with oil in the process.

Roast for about 45 minutes until golden and tender. Drizzle with honey and scatter with the cumin seeds, then turn gently to redistribute and roast for 5–10 minutes more until sticky and caramelised.

CHARRED ASPARAGUS & LEEKS
WITH SAFFRON & PAPRIKA ROUILLE

The magic here lies in the contrasting textures of tender roast asparagus versus crispy shreds of fried leek and a rich base of sweet, smoky rouille. If you don't have time to make it from scratch, cheat the sauce by stirring a pinch of steeped saffron stamens, smoked paprika and crushed garlic into a very good mayonnaise with a dash of lemon juice.

Serves 4 as a side or starter
Preparation time: 20 minutes
Cooking time: 30 minutes

30g (2oz/scant ¼ cup) blanched
    hazelnuts
4 tbsp mild olive oil
1 small leek, trimmed and sliced into
    fine 5cm (2in) long shreds
½ tsp hot smoked paprika
250g (9oz) asparagus spears, trimmed
1 tbsp Dukkah (page 183) or
    ready-made
1 tsp oregano leaves
150g (5oz) Saffron & Paprika Rouille
    (page 173) (see intro)
sea salt and freshly ground
    black pepper

Preheat the oven to 170°C fan (190°C/375°F/gas 5). Tip the hazelnuts onto a baking sheet and roast for 7–8 minutes until golden. Leave to cool slightly, then roughly chop and set aside.

Put half the oil in a frying pan (skillet) and add the leek shreds with a pinch of salt. Fry gently until crisp, taking care not to over-brown them. Drain on paper towels, then dust with paprika.

Increase the oven temperature to 180°C fan (200°C/400°F/gas 6).

Toss the asparagus with the remaining olive oil. Season with salt and pepper and spread on a baking sheet in a single layer. Roast for 15 minutes or so, depending on thickness, until tender and beginning to brown.

Combine the chopped hazelnuts with the dukkah and oregano leaves.

To serve, spoon the rouille onto a platter to form a base and artfully cover with the asparagus, crisp leeks and hazelnut mixture.

BAKED RED ONION PETALS
WITH GRAIN MUSTARD VINAIGRETTE

These sweet and tender roast onion 'petals' can be more than a side if you wish. See them as the start of a warm salad, tossing them – and a little more Grain Mustard Vinaigrette – with wedges of roast beetroot, diced goats' cheese, cooked lentils, pomegranate arials and chicory leaves. Or simply tumble them through a couple of handfuls of rocket (arugula). As they are, they'll go in sandwiches and on pizzas or can be served on the side at barbecues and Sunday roasts. A year-round faithful.

Serves 6 as a side, 4 as a salad base
Preparation time: 10 minutes
Cooking time: 1 hour
Vegan

4 tbsp olive oil
10 small red onions, trimmed
  and halved
1 tbsp red wine vinegar
4 rosemary sprigs, leaves stripped
sea salt and freshly ground
  black pepper
3–4 tbsp Grain Mustard Vinaigrette
  (see page 175) (optional)

Preheat the oven to 170°C fan (190°C/375°F/gas 5). Drizzle the base of a large roasting tin with 2 tablespoons of the olive oil and season with salt and pepper. Sit the halved red onions on the oil, cut-sides down. They should be packed quite snugly in a single layer.

Brush the tops with a further tablespoon of the olive oil, cover tightly with kitchen foil and roast for about 40 minutes until softened and starting to turn golden underneath. Uncover and roast for a further 10 minutes. The top layers of onion should be coming away.

Use the back of a wooden spoon to crush the onions slightly; they should begin to separate into layers or petals. Drizzle with the remaining tablespoon of olive oil and the vinegar, then stir in the rosemary leaves. Return to the oven for 10 minutes until caramelised and sticky.

If you intend to dress the onions with vinaigrette, transfer to serving platter and spoon over 3–4 tablespoons to taste.

SPICED POTATOES & MUSTARD GREENS

A word of warning here: if your chillies happen to be on the hot side, make sure your kitchen is well ventilated. Sizzling mustard seeds and fiery chillies can make for a potent atmosphere! When it comes to greens, a variety of shredded leaves will work, but they must have substance and character; baby spinach isn't the best choice. Instead, try mature spinach leaves, chard, kale, winter or spring greens, mustard greens or beetroot leaves. To make this into a full supper, serve with salted yogurt, chutneys – mango, fresh coconut and coriander (cilantro), lime pickle – and perhaps a simple dhal, plus rice or poppadums.

Serves 4 as a side
Preparation time: 15 minutes
Cooking time: 20 minutes
Vegan

500g (1lb 2oz) Cypriot or other
   waxy potatoes (such as Charlotte),
   scrubbed and cut into 1cm
   (½in) pieces
1 garlic clove, crushed
a thumb of ginger root, peeled and
   finely grated
a small thumb of fresh turmeric,
   peeled and finely grated or ½ tsp
   ground turmeric
2–3 tbsp groundnut (peanut) oil
½ tsp nigella or black onion seeds
1 tsp brown or yellow mustard seeds
2 red or green chillies, finely sliced
1 tsp brown sugar (any kind will do)
400g (14oz) characterful greens,
   roughly shredded (see intro)
½ lime or ½ small lemon
sea salt and freshly ground
   black pepper

Put the potatoes in a large saucepan. Cover with cold water, add a couple of teaspoons of salt and place over a high heat to come up to the boil. Reduce the heat down to medium and simmer briskly for about 14 minutes until the potatoes are just tender to the point of a knife. Drain in a colander and set aside.

Meanwhile, combine the garlic, ginger and turmeric in a small bowl with a splash of water.

Heat a large wok or frying pan (skillet) with 2 tablespoons of the groundnut oil over a medium–high heat. Add the nigella seeds and cook for 30 seconds, then add the ginger mixture with the chillies and cook for about 1 minute until fragrant. Stir in the sugar and cook for around 30 seconds until everything is starting to brown. If the pan looks dry, add the remaining tablespoon of oil, then tip in the drained potatoes and cook, stirring often, for about 4 minutes until just starting to turn golden. Turn the heat to its highest setting, add the greens and continue to stir-fry until they are just-wilted and frazzling at the edges. This should take 2–3 minutes. Season with salt and pepper to taste, adding a squeeze of lemon or lime juice for balance.

DELICATE CRESS & HERB SALAD
WITH SHALLOT & RADISH

For those who enjoy growing their own salads and herbs in window boxes or vegetable plots, this is a spring or summer celebration. It is not so much a recipe as a reminder of the value of exceptional, delicate produce and the simplicity it deserves. Taking the care to shave and slice delicate watermelon and French radishes, the sweetest shallots and the characterful shoots and herbs that make a seasonal salad exquisite matters enormously and is not pretentious.

Use a mandolin to slice the shallots or sweet onions and radishes if you have one, first peeling the radishes if you are using larger varieties with tougher skins, such as watermelon or blue moon. To retain the spirit whilst widening the scope, add young summer herb leaves, such as baby basil and mint, chervil, dill, pea shoots, nasturtium leaves and flowers, chive flowers and tarragon sprigs with shaved candy beetroot, fennel, celery, cucumber, summer squash or carrot.

Serve excellent bread and the freshest young vegetarian cheeses alongside: a grassy goats' cheese, a burrata or buffalo mozzarella, a young Pecorino or any ricotta-type or curd cheese would be fitting.

Serves 4 as a side
Preparation time: 20 minutes
Vegan if served without cheese

100g (3½oz) sweet, young shallots
   or halved sweet white onions,
   sliced paper-thin
100g (3½oz) radishes, peeled if
   the skins are tough and sliced
   paper-thin
a large pinch of unrefined caster
   (superfine) sugar
a pinch of sea salt flakes
1 tbsp best white wine or white
   balsamic vinegar
3–4 tbsp best extra virgin olive oil
2 large handfuls of snipped cress,
   such as red radish, celery, red
   frill mustard, mizuna, sorrel and
   rocket (arugula)
a small handful of micro or baby
   herbs, such as basil, coriander
   (cilantro) and chervil

Put the sliced shallots and radishes in a non-reactive mixing bowl with the sugar and salt, tossing to mix. Set aside to marinate for 5 minutes; the sugar and salt will dissolve. Add the vinegar and 3 tablespoons of the olive oil to the bowl with the snipped cress and herb leaves. Toss through gently, then plate up drizzled with a little more oil.

GREEK-INSPIRED BAKED BUTTER BEANS

I have previously developed and had published a recipe for slow-baked, plump gigantes beans (basically enormous butter (lima) beans) with sweet vegetables, dill and a beautiful olive oil-tomato sauce. It remains one of my ultimate favourites and was heavily inspired by summer days on Greek islands. The only issue with it is the sheer time it takes to make properly, and the difficulty of sourcing dried gigantes beans to cook from scratch, which, at the time of writing, have to be ordered online if you don't happen to live in a major city such as London. This quicker version retains the spirit of that recipe, but uses fat, jarred butter beans. You won't find them at most corner stores, but they are widely available in large supermarkets and health food shops. At a pinch, you could certainly make the recipe with smaller, tinned butter beans. As shown, you can use these intensely flavourful beans as a filling for crisp-skinned baked potatoes with a bitter leaf salad or try them spooned onto griddled toast with pesto, showered with feta and eaten with rice and green vegetables, or served as part of a mezze-type spread with falafel, roast vegetables, flatbread and dips.

Serves 4 as a side
Preparation time: 15 minutes
Cooking time: 1 hour
Vegan if served without yogurt

1 red onion, finely chopped
1 large carrot, finely chopped
1 small fennel bulb, finely chopped
100ml (3½fl oz/scant ½ cup) extra
    virgin olive oil
3 garlic cloves, finely chopped
2 tbsp sundried tomato purée (paste)
2 × 400g (14oz) tins of finely
    chopped tomatoes
½ cinnamon stick
700g (1lb 9oz) jar butter (lima)
    beans, drained
1½ tsp dried oregano
3 tbsp finely chopped dill fronds
sea salt and freshly ground
    black pepper

To serve
4 large baked potatoes
a red chicory (Belgian endive) and
    rocket (arugula) salad
Greek yogurt

Preheat the oven to 160°C fan (180°C/350°F/gas 4).

Soften the onion, carrot and fennel in the oil over a low heat, adding a large pinch of salt to encourage the water out of them. Cook for about 15 minutes, stirring often, until translucent and sweet. Add the garlic, tomato purée, chopped tomatoes and cinnamon stick and cook down for a further 10 minutes to thicken. Add the beans, oregano and half the dill. Transfer to a baking dish, cover with kitchen foil and bake for 30 minutes or so until caramelised at the edges. Season to taste with salt and pepper, remove the cinnamon and scatter with the remaining dill.

To serve as in the picture, spoon into hot, split potatoes that you have first baked with salt and a dash of olive oil. Accompany with a dressed chicory and rocket salad and spoonfuls of thick Greek yogurt.

THE SAUCE

I don't believe we give sauces enough credit or reverence in vegetarian cookery. Hence The Sauce is so much more than an afterthought and is definitely deserving of both its definite article and its own chapter.

Curiously perhaps, given the vegetable-based nature of my recipes, I was first inspired – some years ago – by the distinctly non-vegetarian Pitt Cue Co.'s *The Cookbook*. Sauces are used to elevate and transform dishes throughout that excellent and quirky, flavour-filled book. I am very taken with the idea that vegetarian dishes deserve the same care and pizzaz, even if more thought has to be given to sources of umami and layers of flavour. If a great vegetarian-friendly sauce, pickle, ferment, spice mix, aioli, rouille or mayonnaise can take something as pedestrian as a so-so sandwich or bruschetta and make it indescribably good, just think what a difference those exceptional condiments can make when the food you're anointing them with is already something special. This layering of flavours and attention to varied textures and temperatures is how you set your cooking apart, giving it charisma. For example, sweet and caramelised but plain roasted vegetables can be given a totally different spin and spirit if you shower them with a smoked almond Dukkah and serve them with a Piri Piri Everything sauce or a Saffron & Paprika Rouille. Have fun with this and let your cooking personality shine.

Having said all that, I am a realistic cook when it comes to practicalities, so I have tried to strike a balance. Threading these sauces through the book has been carefully thought through, but it inevitably adds extra work. You'll often (not always) find a recipe directing you to this chapter as an optional extra or, occasionally, as a pivotal part of the main recipe. I'd hate that to feel like a trap for the unsuspecting reader, so not only do these extras tend to be simple as well as impactful, but I have tried to always suggest an alternative if you are short on time or motivation. Think nothing of using these ideas as inspiration for buying a similar product you love and using that instead. A fresh pesto, any great sauerkraut, crisp chilli oil, fresh vegetable pickle or a bought dukkah spice mix, for example. Many ideas here can be improved or cheated quite easily. A fresh, homemade Herb Mayonnaise will be infinitely superior (truthfully, a homemade mayo is the only type I actually like), but instead of whisking your own from scratch, you could certainly buy a good-quality mayonnaise, folding in the chopped herbs, lemon zest, chilli or garlic to match the recipe. You may need to do this anyway to make a recipe vegan-friendly. Your kitchen, your time, your choice.

Many of the recipes in this chapter are so straightforward and quick that it would be a travesty not to try them as written. What could be simpler than stirring tahini paste and miso together, thinning with a dash of warm water and flavouring with aromatics such as ginger, garlic or citrus to make a sauce, a dip or a dressing for falafel, grain bowls or salads?

I encourage you to get behind the importance and ethos of The Sauce in vegetarian food. But I'd like you to take that way of thinking a step further: batch-make these exceptional condiments to fill your fridge and store cupboard, then spoon them over everything.

PINK PICKLES

The prettiest of pickles and so simple to make; this is a quick version to be stored in the fridge. You'll want to eat them on everything so there's little point in potting them up properly. If you want the pickling liquid to be brighter, use unrefined sugar, but I prefer to add a little caramel flavour.

You can make any number of variations to these pickles to suit your taste. To make a red onion and radish version, swap out some of the sliced red onion for finely sliced raw radishes. To make a pinker still red onion and beetroot version, swap out some red onions for raw beetroot slices. Regarding aromatics, you could fragrance the latter version with whole black peppercorns and bay leaves, added to the onions. Or try using fennel or coriander seeds or juniper berries. A few fine slices of fresh ginger and/or chilli are good when using as a perky taco or guacamole topping.

Makes about 700g (1lb 9oz) or 2 jars
Preparation time: 15 minutes
Pickling time: 1–2 days
Vegan

For the pickling liquid
150g (5oz/heaped ¾ cup) light soft
   brown sugar
1 tsp sea salt flakes
150ml (5fl oz/scant ⅔ cup) red
   wine vinegar

Ingredients for the basic version
600g (1lb 5oz) small red onions,
   halved and finely sliced

**Alternative for a red onion and
radish version**
450g (1lb) small red onions, halved
   and finely sliced
150g (5oz) raw radishes, finely sliced

**Alternative for a red onion and
beetroot version**
400g (14oz) small red onions, halved
   and finely sliced
200g (7oz) candy or standard
   beetroots (beets), peeled and finely
   shaved or sliced
1 tbsp whole black peppercorns
3 bay leaves or 1 tsp fennel or
   coriander seeds or juniper berries

Aromatics
a few fine slices of fresh ginger root
   and/or chilli (optional)

Mix the sugar and salt into the vinegar.

Pack the sliced red onion (and radish or beetroot, if using) into two clean, lidded jars or a plastic container, adding any aromatics you like the sound of – or none if you don't. Pour the pickling liquid over, dividing between the two jars, if using. Cover tightly and chill. Keep in the fridge for at least a day before using, preferably 2 days, and use up within 4–6 weeks.

CHIMICHURRI

An Argentinian-inspired flavour kick to spoon over, dress or dip into. I use this everywhere – it's perfect as an accompaniment to barbecued or griddled vegetables, as a punchy salad dressing, on slow-roasted aubergines or with grilled halloumi kebabs. Swap the coriander out for double the parsley, or even a less-traditional mixture of parsley and mint, if preferred.

Makes about 400ml (13fl oz/generous 1½ cups)
Preparation time: 25 minutes
Vegan

1 tsp cumin seeds (lightly crushed)
4 garlic cloves, chopped
4 red chillies, chopped
½ tsp sea salt flakes
a small bunch of coriander (cilantro) with stalks, chopped
a small bunch of flat-leaf parsley with stalks, chopped
1 tbsp fresh oregano leaves, chopped
90ml (3fl oz/generous ⅓ cup) red wine vinegar
120ml (4fl oz/½ cup) extra virgin olive oil
sea salt and freshly ground black pepper

Put the cumin seeds in a dry frying pan (skillet) set over a medium heat and toast, tossing the pan now and then for 1–2 minutes until fragrant and a touch darker in colour. Crush lightly in a pestle and mortar or with the base of a sturdy jar on a chopping board.

Pound the garlic, chillies, salt and herbs together in a pestle and mortar until a rough paste forms, stirring in the vinegar, oil and 2 tablespoons of water with the crushed cumin seeds, tasting and adjusting the seasoning with salt and pepper as needed. It will certainly need black pepper, but shouldn't require any or much salt.

To make in a mini food processor, put all the ingredients in the bowl with 2 tablespoons of water and pulse until a rough paste forms. Stir in the cumin and taste for seasoning, adjusting as needed.

Use straight away or put in a lidded jar and keep in the fridge for up to 2 days, stirring well before use.

CHILLI-PEPPER JAM

As with most things in this chapter, you'll want to spoon this sweet and hot jam (it's far less sickly than the name implies) over everything. It's light on sugar and big on bright flavour so won't keep for weeks. Store it in the fridge and add to every sandwich, toasted or not, or eat with cheese.

Makes 400g (14oz)
Preparation time: 15 minutes
Cooking time: 40 minutes
Vegan

3 tbsp olive oil
8 garlic cloves, finely chopped
5 red chillies, trimmed and sliced
2 large red (bell) peppers, deseeded and finely sliced
1 tsp fennel seeds
400g (14oz) tin of plum tomatoes, snipped with scissors in the tin
3 tbsp unrefined granulated sugar
60ml (2fl oz/¼ cup) red wine vinegar
1 tsp sea salt

Put the oil in a large saucepan set over a low heat. Add the garlic, chillies, peppers and fennel seeds and cook, stirring, for 15–20 minutes until very soft and just beginning to caramelise slightly.

Stir in the tomatoes, sugar, vinegar and salt. Turn the heat up to medium–high and simmer to reduce the mixture down for a further 20 minutes or so, stirring almost constantly towards the end to stop it catching on the base of the pan. It should be sticky and thick. Leave to cool, then spoon into in a clean jar or container with a lid or cover. Store in the fridge for up to 2 weeks.

From left:
Chilli-pepper Jam (page 169),
Fragrant Chilli Oil (page 172),
Chimichurri (page 169) and
Pink Pickles (page 168).

FRAGRANT CHILLI OIL
WITH GINGER, SHALLOTS & GARLIC

Spoon over broths, salads, dumplings, roasts, rice, noodles, avocado toast … you'll be addicted. If you can't find salted black beans to add that hum of umami, leave them out or stir in a tablespoon of miso paste with the sugar at the end. You can go a little further here and turn the oil temperature up towards the end, further crisping the aromatic ingredients. I have left them greatly condensed but with a little chew. Just be aware that the garlic can catch and play it safe.

Makes 2 × 350g (12oz) jars
Preparation time: 30 minutes
Cooking time: 35 minutes
Vegan

300ml (10fl oz/1¼ cups) groundnut (peanut) oil
200g (7oz) mild red chillies, finely sliced
2 tbsp dried chilli (hot pepper) flakes
2 garlic bulbs, cloves peeled and sliced
300g (10½oz) (about 6) shallots, halved and sliced
150g (5oz) ginger root, peeled and finely chopped
30g (12oz) fresh turmeric, peeled and chopped or 1½ tsp ground turmeric
2 lemongrass stalks, trimmed and sliced
1½ tbsp sea salt flakes
10g (½oz) Chinese salted black beans, finely chopped (optional)
2½ tbsp light soft brown sugar

Put the oil in a large saucepan with all the ingredients except the black beans and the sugar and set over a low heat. Gently bring the temperature of the oil up to 105°C (220°F), adjusting the heat on the hob if you need to, but keeping it as low as possible. If you don't have a thermometer, guess this by bringing the oil up to a temperature at which the aromatics gently 'simmer' and fizz, but don't fry too briskly. Simmer for 20 minutes until the chopped ingredients are greatly reduced in volume, having lost much of their water. Stir it often during this time.

Stir in the black beans, if using, and keep the oil fizzing gently for another 15 minutes, stirring until the ingredients in the oil are golden and reduced right down.

Carefully stir in the sugar and remove from the heat. Leave to cool in the pan for 20 minutes, stirring occasionally.

Pot up in clean jars (from a hot dishwasher is best), cover and keep in a cool, dry place. It'll keep for a couple of months at least, but don't leave it too much longer as the aromatics lose their fragrance a bit. Once opened, it's safest to store the oil in the fridge. It'll keep for weeks.

SAFFRON
& PAPRIKA ROUILLE

A sweet, garlicky, rich, sun-warmed something to dip raw vegetables into. A rouille is essentially an aioli with bells on, often made with breadcrumbs, always spiked with saffron and generally destined for a bowl of bouillabaisse. I'd suggest you serve it with bread and any of the fulsome roasted vegetable soups in this book or spread it on toast to top with roast fennel and peppers. The flavours are also wonderful with whole roasted tomatoes, stuffed with saffron rice.

Makes 300g (10½oz)
Preparation time: 25 minutes

a pinch of saffron stamens
2 garlic cloves, crushed
300ml (10fl oz/2¼ cups) mild olive oil
2 egg yolks
½ tsp sea salt flakes
finely grated zest and juice of
    1 small lemon
½ tsp smoked paprika
salt and freshly ground black pepper

In a small bowl or mug, soak the saffron stamens in 1 tablespoon of just-boiled water for 10 minutes.

Put the garlic in a mixing bowl with the egg yolks, salt, lemon zest and half the juice. Whisk with a balloon whisk until thick and smooth. Whilst whisking constantly, slowly drizzle in the remaining oil in a steady stream. The mixture should look thick, glossy and smooth.

Whisk in the remaining lemon juice and the saffron in its soaking water. Season to taste and stir in the paprika. You should have a thick but spoonable mayonnaise sauce. Use straight away or cover and chill for up to 4 days.

From top left:
Grain Mustard Vinaigrette (opposite),
Summer Herb Seed Pesto (opposite),
Piri Piri Everything (page 176) and
Saffron & Paprika Rouille (page 173).

SUMMER HERB & SEED PESTO

Make this with all basil, as is traditional or use a combination of herbs. You could also include Greek basil, chervil or chives.

Makes about 300g (10½oz)
Preparation time: 20 minutes

60g (2oz/½ cup) sunflower seeds
2 garlic cloves, roughly chopped
a large pinch of sea salt flakes
a handful of basil leaves, chopped
a handful of mint leaves, chopped
a handful of parsley leaves, chopped
about 120ml (4fl oz/½ cup) extra virgin olive oil, plus extra to cover
25g (1oz) vegetarian Parmesan-style cheese, finely grated

Start by placing the sunflower seeds in a frying pan (skillet) set over a medium heat. Toast, shaking the pan often, for 2–3 minutes until fragrant and very lightly browned. Set aside.

To make in the traditional style, use a pestle and mortar. Start by pounding the garlic with a pinch of sea salt to make a paste, then gradually add the herbs and sunflower seeds. Keep pounding together as you add the olive oil in a steady stream. Be mindful not to turn the herb leaves to sludge and only stir in the cheese at the end.

To make it in a small processor, start with the garlic and a good pinch of sea salt. Blitz to chop, then add the herbs and blitz again. Scrape down the sides and throw in the sunflower seeds with a good glug of olive oil. Pulse, dribbling olive oil into the processor with the blades still moving to make a bright-green, textured paste, then stir in the cheese.

To store, spoon the pesto into a jar, level the top and cover with a thin layer of olive oil, followed by the jar lid. It will keep in the fridge for a week or so.

GRAIN MUSTARD VINAIGRETTE

A classic sharp and chic vinaigrette to dress everything from crunchy lettuce to bitter leaves, pulses, massaged kale and steamed green vegetables.

Makes 200ml (7fl oz/scant 1 cup)
Preparation time: 10 minutes
Vegan

3 small shallots, very finely chopped
2 heaped tsp wholegrain mustard
½ tsp unrefined caster (superfine) sugar
4 tbsp red or white wine vinegar
½ garlic clove, crushed
100ml (3½fl oz/scant ½ cup) extra virgin olive oil
5 tbsp mild olive oil
3 tbsp very finely chopped parsley leaves or chives (optional)
a few drops of lemon juice (optional)
sea salt and freshly ground black pepper

Soak the chopped shallots in a bowl of cool water for 10 minutes, then tip into a sieve and rinse thoroughly under the cold tap. Drain well.

Combine the drained shallots with the mustard, sugar, vinegar and garlic in a bowl, seasoning with salt and pepper. Gradually whisk in the extra virgin olive oil to emulsify, adding a tablespoon of cold water once the extra virgin olive oil has been incorporated. Continue to whisk in the remaining mild olive oil, then season to taste and stir in the chopped herbs, if using. You may wish to add a dash of lemon juice, too, according to your own taste.

PIRI PIRI EVERYTHING

This addictive Portugese-inspired chilli sauce gained its name because you'll want to spoon it over everything. I particularly love it over roasted vegetables. It freezes well in an airtight box or ice cube tray for up to 3 months so you may want to double the recipe. This quantity keeps very well in a sealed jar in the fridge for a couple of weeks, provided the surface is covered with oil to protect it from oxidising.

Makes about 350ml (12¼fl oz/ 1½ cups)
Preparation time: 25 minutes
Cooking time: 10 minutes
Vegan

2 large red (bell) peppers
5 large red chillies
1 small red onion, chopped
2 large garlic cloves, chopped
2 red piri piri or birdseye chillies, chopped
5 tbsp extra virgin olive oil
1 tbsp hot smoked paprika
2 tsp dried oregano
2 tbsp red wine vinegar
½ tbsp sea salt flakes
½ tsp black pepper
finely grated zest and juice of 1 large lemon

Start by charring the whole peppers and chillies on a baking sheet under a hot grill (broiler) for 10 minutes, turning every few minutes, until blackened and blistered all over. Transfer to a bowl, cover with a plate and set aside to steam for 15 minutes. Peel as best you can (don't be too fastidious here), then cut the peppers and chillies open and remove the seeds and stalks.

Pulse the red onion, garlic and birdseye chillies in a mini food processor until quite finely chopped. Add the charred peppers and chillies with the olive oil, paprika, oregano, red wine vinegar, salt, pepper, lemon zest and lemon juice. Pulse again to make a rough paste, then transfer to a clean jar, cover with a lid and store in the fridge for up to 2 weeks.

TARRAGON & CORNICHON AIOLI

This extremely boisterous aioli will keep covered in the fridge for a few days. You may wish to lighten it up with a spoonful or two of Greek yogurt, but I love its garlic and tarragon hum as-is. You can, of course, cheat by stirring the tarragon, chopped cornichons and crushed garlic into 400g (14oz), or a jar, of good-quality bought mayonnaise with a squeeze of lemon juice to brighten.

Makes a 400g (14oz) jar
Preparation time: 25 minutes
Vegan

2 large egg yolks
a pinch of salt
5 tbsp best extra virgin olive oil
330ml (11¼fl oz/1⅓ cups) mild olive oil
juice of ½ lemon
1 garlic clove, crushed
a small bunch of tarragon, finely chopped
60g (2oz) drained cornichons, finely diced

Put the egg yolks in a large, high-sided mixing bowl set on top of a damp tea (dish) towel to stop it moving around. Start whisking the egg yolks with a pinch of salt to break them down.

Being very cautious and only adding it a drop at a time at first, begin to drip the extra virgin olive oil into the egg yolks as you whisk constantly. Keep whisking and dripping the oil in – your arm will ache – until all the extra virgin is incorporated, then move on to the mild oil, adding it in exactly the same way. As the aioli begins to thicken up, you can begin to add the oil in a very fine stream, but you mustn't stop whisking or the mixture could curdle. Once thick and wobbly, fold in the lemon juice, crushed garlic, tarragon and cornichons with a fat pinch of salt to taste. You may want to add a dash more lemon juice. Use straight away or transfer to a clean jar, cover and chill until needed. It will keep in the fridge for up to 5 days.

CHARRED PICKLES

Superlative jars of pickled Mediterranean vegetables that have first been griddled for extra flavour. The vegetables are sweet-sour, crunchy and utterly delicious by themselves or as an accompaniment to endless dip, sandwich, salad plate and cheeseboard variations. Swap out herbs and spices as you like: thyme for oregano, coriander seeds for the fennel seeds, for example.

To sterilise your jars and lids and any utensils you'll use to fill them, either run them through the hot cycle of a dishwasher or put them in a saucepan, cover with boiling water from the kettle and place over a low heat to simmer for 10–15 minutes. Drain and leave to dry before using.

Makes two 1 litre (34fl oz/4 cup) jars
Preparation time: 30 minutes including sterilising
Cooking time: 30 minutes
Vegan

1 aubergine (eggplant), trimmed
2 medium courgettes (zucchini), trimmed
2 large red (bell) peppers, deseeded and halved
4 small shallots, halved
2 tbsp olive oil
1 mild red chilli, sliced
3 oregano or marjoram sprigs, leaves stripped
2 tsp brown or yellow mustard seeds
1 tbsp fennel seeds
50g (1¾oz) salt
50g (1¾oz) unrefined caster (superfine) sugar
500ml (17fl oz/2 cups) white wine vinegar

Using the introduction note for guidance, sterilise two 1 litre (34fl oz/4 cup) heatproof jars with tight-fitting lids.

Cut the trimmed aubergine, courgettes and peppers into chubby wedges and spears that are about 6cm (2¼in) long.

Toss all the vegetables including the shallots with the olive oil in a bowl. Place a griddle pan over a high heat until smoking. Griddle the oiled vegetables in a single layer, in batches, for about 2–3 minutes on each side. They should be well-coloured with grill marks but still holding their shape. Once charred enough, they should release from the pan quite easily to turn over. Remove to a platter as they are cooked.

Divide the griddled vegetables between the two jars, packing them in very tightly, adding the chilli slices, oregano leaves, mustard seeds and fennel seeds as you go. Add half the salt and half the sugar to each jar. Combine the vinegar with 250ml (9fl oz/1 cup) water and divide this between the jars. Close the lids tightly and give them a good shake.

Place the jars in the fridge and leave for at least 48 hours before using, shaking now and then. You can use a cool store cupboard to store them instead; the fridge is just an extra insurance policy in case your jar sterilising didn't work perfectly. Ideally, you'd leave the vegetables to pickle for longer so that their flavours deepen and develop; they will get better and better for up to 6 weeks and will keep for up to 12 weeks in the fridge or a cool, dark cupboard.

Clockwise from left:
Beetroot Sauerkraut (page 181),
Tarragon & Cornichon Aioli (page 176),
Pickled Carrots (page 182) and
Tahini-Miso Sauce (page 182).

Clockwise from left:
Basil & Lemon Pistou (page 180),
Charred Pickles (page 177), Dukkah (page 183)
and Herb Mayonnaise (page 180).

HERB MAYONNAISE

The soft herbs you use are up to you, but you can easily vary this further by stirring in some finely grated lemon zest and/or chopped chilli and/or crushed toasted coriander or fennel seeds.

Makes 520ml (18fl oz/generous 2 cups)
Preparation time: 15 minutes

2 large egg yolks
a pinch of salt
1 heaped teaspoon Dijon mustard
2 tbsp white wine vinegar
500ml (17fl oz/2 cups) groundnut (peanut)
    or other mild oil
juice of ½ lemon
a large handful of soft summer herbs such as basil, mint,
    chives and flat-leaf parsley in any combination, finely
    chopped

Using a balloon whisk or, to save your arm, hand-held electric beaters, whisk the egg yolks and salt in a bowl.

Add the mustard and a teaspoon of vinegar, whisking non-stop to blend thoroughly. Starting drop by drop as you whisk continuously, gradually add the oil. Progress to a very fine dribble, never letting up on the whisking as you add about half the oil.

Now add another 2 teaspoons of vinegar, whisking in, of course, then continue to dribble and whisk in the remaining oil. By this time the mixture will have thickened significantly and should be taking on a wobbly, mayonnaise-like consistency.

Season with a pinch of salt, a squeeze of lemon juice and the remaining tablespoon of vinegar. Stir in the chopped herbs of your choice, adding any extras suggested in the introduction. Use straight away or store in a clean, lidded container in the fridge for up to 5 days.

BASIL & LEMON PISTOU

A vegan pesto, really. All the flavour, but none of the dairy. Add chopped red or green chilli at the end or replace some of the basil with mint or parsley.

Makes about 250ml (9fl oz/1 cup)
Preparation time: 15 minutes
Vegan

2 garlic cloves, roughly chopped
a large pinch of sea salt flakes
a large bunch of basil leaves, chopped
about 170ml (6fl oz/¾ cup) best-quality extra virgin olive
    oil, plus extra to cover
finely grated zest and juice of 1 small lemon

To make this in the traditional style, pound the garlic cloves and a pinch of sea salt to a paste in a pestle and mortar, then gradually add the basil, pounding together, but mindful not to turn the herb leaves to sludge. Gradually add the olive oil in a steady stream, pounding all the time. Stir in the lemon zest and juice.

To make it in a small processor, start with the garlic and a good pinch of sea salt. Blitz to chop, then add the basil and blitz again. Add a good glug of oil, scrape down the sides and pulse, dribbling olive oil into the processor with the blades still moving to make a bright-green, textured paste. Stir in the lemon zest and juice.

To store, spoon the pistou into a jar, level the top and cover with a thin layer of olive oil, followed by the jar lid. It will keep in the fridge for a couple of days, though not as long as a pesto because of the lemon juice, which will affect the basil's green colour.

BEETROOT SAUERKRAUT

Let's be upfront about the smell of cultured cabbage … the fragrance as it ferments isn't indicative of its vibrant taste and crunch, or its digestive benefits. Encouraging so-called 'good' bacteria to break down cruciferous vegetables inevitably produces a sulphurous odour and if you've tried sauerkraut, you'll know whether you're a fan of its fizzy-salty nature. Nurture a love for this type of sour, fermented food and you'll enhance the variety of good digestive bacteria in your gut, whilst adding oomph to sandwiches, salads and cheese plates.

Makes about 1kg (2lb 4oz)
Preparation time: 30 minutes
Curing time: 4 days
Vegan

550g (1lb 4oz) red cabbage, finely shredded
2 tsp sea salt flakes
350g (12oz) beetroot (beets), scrubbed and finely shredded
1 small pear, scrubbed and coarsely grated, discarding the core
1 tsp finely grated ginger root
1 small garlic clove, crushed
½ tsp caraway seeds or fennel seeds
bottled water or boiled and cooled water, if needed

Sterilise a 1kg (2lb 4oz) Kilner (Mason) jar by running it through the hot cycle of a dishwasher or by washing in hot soapy water and drying in a low oven.

Put on some clean rubber or surgical gloves; red cabbage and beetroot stain fingers terribly. Put the shredded cabbage in a bowl with the salt and massage by hand for a few minutes to break it down and soften it, then leave it to sit for 10 minutes. Add the beetroot and massage for a couple of minutes more. Mix in the grated pear, ginger, garlic and the caraway or fennel seeds (your choice). The mixture should be juicy, as massaging with salt will have released a lot of water from the vegetables. Transfer the whole lot to the sterilised jar, packing down tightly and topping up the liquid with water to just cover, if needed.

Culture at cool room temperature in a dark spot for 4–5 days, turning the jar now and then. The cultured sauerkraut should look fizzy and softened. Transfer the closed jar to the fridge. The longer it stays out of the fridge at the culturing stage, the more sour the sauerkraut becomes, so the timings are a matter of personal taste. This is a sweetish mixture due to the beetroot and pear but play it safe if you don't love a strong cabbage taste. Once refrigerated and kept that way, the kraut will keep for a few months, becoming pleasingly more sour as time passes. Make sure to secure the lid very tightly after opening as the aroma of sauerkraut isn't quite as delicious as the taste.

TAHINI-MISO SAUCE

Serve this as a thick and intensely flavoured condiment. Or whisk in warm water to make a creamy dressing for noodle salads and falafel. Stir spoonfuls into mayonnaise – preferably a Japanese-style mayo such as Kewpie – to make a savoury dip or a spread for bao buns or Vietnamese-style *banh mi* sandwiches. To change the flavour, add finely chopped garlic, chilli, chives or coriander (cilantro) or stir in toasted sesame seeds.

Makes 150g (4oz)
Preparation time: 5 minutes
Vegan

120g (4oz) tahini, stirred
3 tbsp white miso paste
juice of 1 lemon
2 tsp finely grated ginger root
alternative flavourings (optional) (see intro)

Combine all the ingredients in a bowl. Then let down with warm water to make the consistency you prefer, adding it a tablespoon at a time, to make a condiment, dressing or dip.

PICKLED CARROTS

An addictive and quick pickle, perfect for adding to Vietnamese or Thai-style salads and sandwiches or to accompany stir-fries, dumplings and bao buns. Make sure you sterilise the jar you use thoroughly; the easiest way is to run it and its lid through a hot dishwasher cycle. Alternatively, wash in hot soapy water and dry out in a moderate oven for 15 minutes.

Makes two 400g (14oz) jars
Preparation time: 15 minutes
Vegan

1 tbsp coriander seeds
500g (1lb 2oz) carrots, peeled and shredded
1 red chilli, sliced
250ml (9fl oz/1 cup) rice wine vinegar
50g (1¾oz/¼ cup) unrefined caster (superfine) sugar
1 tsp sea salt

Toast the coriander seeds in a dry frying pan (skillet) set over a medium heat. They should take a minute or so to become fragrant. Crush lightly, then combine with the carrots, sliced chilli, rice wine vinegar, sugar, salt and 150ml (5fl oz/scant ⅔ cup) of water. Divide between two sterilised 400g (14oz) jars. Screw the sterilised lids on tightly and shake well. Leave in the fridge for at least 4 hours before using. Ideally, you'd leave the pickles for a few days before eating. They will keep, chilled, for a few weeks, but you'll be sure to use them sooner.

DUKKAH

An Egyptian nut, seed and spice mix for everything. You can buy dukkah, of course, but a homemade version is going to be miles better than most and there's the added draw of being able to vary the nuts as you wish (almonds instead of hazelnuts, for example) and the spices (you could add Nigella seeds, chilli (hot pepper) flakes or cayenne). It's used countless times throughout this book, sometimes with alternative nuts and seeds – such as smoked almonds or pumpkin seeds chopped in to this master recipe. Strew it over falafel, hummus, salads, cooked wholegrains and pretty much anything else that could benefit from a toasty, rounded hit of spice and crunch.

Makes about 150g (5oz)
Preparation time: 5 minutes
Cooking time: 15 minutes
Vegan

60g (2oz/scant ½ cup) blanched
    hazelnuts
60g (2oz/scant ½ cup) unsalted shelled
    pistachios
3 tbsp sunflower seeds
4 tbsp sesame seeds
1 tbsp fennel seeds
2 tbsp cumin seeds
5 tbsp coriander seeds
1 tsp sea salt flakes
2 tsp sweet smoked paprika

Preheat the oven to 130°C fan (150°C/300°F/gas 2).

Spread the hazelnuts and pistachios out on a baking sheet and roast for 10 minutes. Scatter the sunflower seeds onto the sheet and return it to the oven for 5 minutes until fragrant and pale golden. Set aside.

Scatter the sesame, fennel, cumin and coriander seeds over the base of a large frying pan (skillet) and set over a low heat. Toast, shaking the pan frequently, for 2–3 minutes, or until the seeds are slightly darker and fragrant. Grind roughly in a pestle and mortar or with the base of a sturdy jar on a chopping board.

Tip the cooled nuts and seeds into a food processor with the ground spices, salt and paprika and blitz to a rough rubble. Transfer to a small airtight jar and keep in a cool place. Try to use within 2 weeks before the flavours have a chance to dull.

THE FINALE

Frankly, I'd rather have a decent apple than a worthy imitation of dessert. I've also taken the liberty of assuming nobody needs a recipe or reminder that chic chocolates with coffee or the ripest seasonal fruit served with ice cream of your choice are always welcome.

So here we have an unashamed chapter of glorious homemade desserts and puddings to round off your kitchen repertoire properly, making this a true go-to book for all occasions. I've played to the crowd with beloved flavour combinations and, as befits the nature of this book, my best and modernised re-imaginings of classics.

The ultimate voluptuous Carrot Cake with a brown butter and cream cheese vanilla frosting … an ingenious vegan Chocolate Mousse with Burnt Sugar … an ethereal Rhubarb, Buttermilk & Cardamom Ice Cream … a Peach & Hazelnut Frangipane Tart of summer dreams. Every single recipe is a winner, whether indulgent or refreshing.

It may seem a contradiction to concentrate an entire book on colourful, fresh, intensely flavoured healthy food, only to finish it off with a chapter of sumptuous desserts, but where a finale is needed for a meal, there is celebration and that can't be stinted on or what would be the point? To take any other attitude would be a compromise and a travesty. It would completely misunderstand the role food has in our lives beyond fuel. I say this as a masters-level nutritionist with a strong belief in high-quality nourishment almost all of the time. But it is just as important to let go and mark that birthday, that party, that anniversary or any other life celebration with food that brings you and the people you love joy. A beloved dessert can form the basis of life-long traditions in families and among friends.

With occasion-cooking in mind, I've made sure every recipe in this chapter can be made ahead in some way. The vast majority can be finished entirely in advance so you'll only need to take them to the table and can relax knowing your grand finale is in the bag, so to speak. A few will need to be plated up or heated up before serving, but you will be able to get all the components prepared well in advance and we're only talking about spooning a pre-chilled cheesecake mixture over a caramelised biscuit crumb or popping a chilled crumble dish into the oven until bubbling at the edges.

SALTED HONEYCOMB CHOCOLATE BROWNIES

This, frankly obscene, brownie recipe is rich, salty (a good thing) and decadent. Since writing its first incarnation over twenty years ago, I've been wheeling versions out at any and all celebrations. It's much requested. Little quirks – such as scattering some of the chocolate chunks across the base of the tin so that they further caramelise on baking – make all the difference. I used to use white chocolate but have now gravitated to 'blonde' for even deeper caramel notes. If you prefer, you can replace some or all of the blonde and dark chocolates with white, milk or dark chocolate in any combination. Chopped pecans or dried cherries will also work in place of the honeycomb; bury these in the batter rather than scattering on top to prevent them catching in the oven. For once, I recommend erring on the smaller side when divvying into portions.

Makes about 16 brownies
Preparation time: 30 minutes
Cooking time: 35 minutes

300g (10½oz) dark chocolate
    (minimum 70% cocoa solids),
    broken into pieces
250g (9oz) unsalted butter
4 large eggs
150g (5oz/⅔ cup) unrefined caster
    (superfine) sugar
150g (5oz/heaped ¾ cup) light brown
    muscovado sugar
2 tsp vanilla extract
120g (4oz/½ cup) plain (all-purpose)
    flour or spelt flour
½ tsp baking powder
¾ tsp sea salt flakes
20g (¾oz/¼ cup) cocoa (unsweetened
    chocolate) powder
200g (7oz) white chocolate,
    roughly chopped
100g (3½oz) honeycomb, broken into
    bite-sized pieces

Preheat the oven to 170°C fan (190°C/375°F/gas 5). Line a 23 × 32cm (9 × 13in) brownie pan with non-stick baking parchment.

Melt 200g (7oz) of the dark chocolate and the butter together in a heatproof bowl set over a pan of simmering water, stirring occasionally. If you can't be bothered with a bain marie, you can do this directly in a saucepan, stirring over the lowest possible heat, but don't leave it alone as the chocolate can scorch easily and ruin the flavour. Once melted, set aside to cool slightly.

Beat the eggs, sugars and vanilla extract together in the bowl of an electric mixer (or using hand-held electric beaters) at high speed for about 3 minutes until thick and increased in volume by about one-third.

Sift the flour, baking powder, ½ tsp salt and the cocoa over the top, then pour in the melted chocolate and butter mixture. Fold together until smooth. Gently fold in about one-third of the remaining dark and white chocolate (mixed together) and about half the honeycomb.

Scatter half the remaining white and dark chocolate over the base of the prepared tin. Spoon the brownie mixture on top, smoothing the top. Scatter with the remaining chocolate and the remaining smashed honeycomb. Finish by scattering with the remaining salt. Slide into the oven and immediately reduce the oven temperature to 160°C fan (180°C/350°F/gas 4). Bake for 35–40 minutes until almost firm in the middle. The mixture should still have a slight 'wobble' in the middle when the pan is jiggled.

Once cool, cut the brownies into around 16 brownies, depending on preference. They will keep in an airtight container for up to 4 days and freeze beautifully.

CHOCOLATE TIRAMISU

A heavenly chocolate version of the marsala and mascarpone classic, spiked with a touch of bitter caramel and Amaretto for balance and dredged with grated chocolate as well as the customary cocoa powder. To make one large tiramisu to serve 6–8, use a 25cm (10in) square ceramic dish with a generous depth. Start with half the coffee-dipped sponge fingers in a single layer, building up as below with a second layer of sponge fingers in the middle, finishing with the final flourish of cocoa and grated chocolate once the tiramisu has been chilled overnight or for a couple of days.

Serves 8
Preparation time: 40 minutes
Chilling time: at least 6 hours
or overnight

200g (7oz/scant 1 cup) unrefined
   caster sugar
250ml (9fl oz/1 cup) espresso-strength
   coffee, cooled
4 tbsp cocoa (unsweetened chocolate)
   powder, sifted
a pinch of salt
3 tbsp Amaretto
150g (5oz) dark chocolate (minimum
   70% cocoa solids), 100g (3½oz)
   chopped and 50g (1¾oz)
   finely grated
350g (12oz) mascarpone
4 large eggs at room temperature,
   separated
100ml (3½fl oz/scant ½ cup) Marsala
   wine
200g (7oz) pack Savoiardi
   sponge fingers

Dredge 50g (1¾oz) of caster sugar evenly over the base of a large frying pan (skillet) set over a low heat to melt the sugar, swirling the pan every now and then so it heats through evenly. Once melted, turn the heat up a notch and allow the caramel to turn a deep amber colour. Add the coffee to the pan, swirling to dissolve the sugar in it. Remove from the heat and add 2 tablespoons of the cocoa powder and the pinch of salt, stirring well until completely smooth. Leave to cool slightly, then stir in the Amaretto and set aside.

Melt the 100g (3½oz) of chopped dark chocolate in a bowl set over, but not touching, a saucepan of simmering water, stirring often until completely melted. Set aside to cool.

The following method is simple, but you will need a few bowls to hand. Put the mascarpone in one mixing bowl and give it a brief whisk to loosen so that it incorporates smoothly later.

Put the 4 egg yolks in a second, large mixing bowl and whisk – with a balloon whisk or with electric beaters – for a few minutes until pale and fluffy. Add 100g (3½oz) of caster sugar and the Marsala, then whisk again until combined. Fold in the cooled melted chocolate and the mascarpone to make a smooth mixture. Preferably using hand-held electric beaters for ease, whisk the whites in another large, clean bowl until they form soft peaks. Add the remaining 50g (1¾oz/¼ cup) of caster sugar and whisk again until stiff and glossy (about 2 minutes). Gently fold the whites into the chocolate mixture using a spatula or large metal spoon to retain as much air as possible.

Have 8 glasses or cups with a 250–300ml (7–10fl oz/1–1¼ cups) capacity ready if you wish to make individual tiramisu. Otherwise, see the recipe introduction for a note on making this in one large dish. Dip each sponge finger into the coffee mixture for a couple of seconds so it absorbs the liquid but doesn't disintegrate. Break in half and sit in the base of each glass or cup, adding an extra tablespoon of coffee mixture to each. Add a little of the finely grated chocolate over each serving to cover. Spoon a generous layer of chocolate-mascarpone mixture on top, to reach almost halfway up each glass. Repeat the dipped biscuit (no extra coffee mixture needs to be drizzled over this time) and grated chocolate layer then cover again with more chocolate-mascarpone to reach the top of each glass.

Rest in the fridge for at least 6 hours, or preferably overnight, so the pudding properly sets and the sponge fingers absorb the coffee evenly. The tiramisu will sit happily for a couple of days before eating. Dredge liberally with the remaining cocoa powder and add the remaining grated dark chocolate on top before serving.

PEDRO XIMÉNEZ SPICED PEARS

The ultimate make-ahead dinner party or Christmas dessert: whole pears, infused and glazed with the richest spiced sherry syrup. They are, perhaps, even lovelier cold than warm. To ring the changes, use a comparably sweet sherry, ruby port, marsala wine or any characterful dessert wine instead of the PX; vary the spices with whole star anise, slices of fresh ginger or green cardamom pods; throw a handful of plump Lexia raisins into the reducing syrup for a variation on rum and raisin.

Serves 4
Preparation time: 15 minutes
Cooking time: 1 hour
**Vegan without the crème fraîche or
    ice cream**

750ml (26fl oz/3 cups) Pedro Ximénez
    sherry (see intro)
1 small cinnamon stick
4 green cardamom pods, bruised
1 vanilla pod (bean), split
2 wide strips of orange zest
100g (3½oz/heaped ½ cup) light
    muscovado sugar
4 medium pears, peeled
crème fraîche or vanilla ice cream,
    to serve

Preheat the oven to 180°C fan (200°C/400°F/gas 6). Have ready an ovenproof dish which will hold the horizontal pears snugly in a single layer. Ideally, it would have a lid, but a double layer of kitchen foil will be fine if not.

Put the sherry in a medium saucepan with the cinnamon, cardamom pods, vanilla pod, orange zest and muscovado sugar. Set over a low heat and slowly bring to the boil, stirring occasionally to dissolve the sugar.

Cut a horizontal slice from the base of each pear so that they'll stand up straight by the end of the recipe. Lay the pears in your chosen dish on their sides, tuck in the whole spices and pour the poaching liquid over to all but submerge the fruit. Keep the saucepan handy for later. Cover the dish with a lid or double layer of kitchen foil, tucking the latter in tightly around the edges. Bake for around 45 minutes, using their stalks to gingerly turn the pears every 10 minutes or so before re-covering. Once cooked, the pears should be tender to the point of a knife but holding their shape firmly.

Using a slotted spoon, set the baked pears aside and strain the poaching liquid back into its original saucepan.

Simmer the pear-poaching liquid down by at least half until glossy and syrupy. Pour back over the pears. Serve each upright warm or chilled pear cloaked with spiced syrup, accompanied with scoops of cool crème fraîche or ice cream.

FLOURLESS CHOCOLATE & CHERRY ROULADE

A rich, squidgy chocolate sponge is spread with chocolate ganache, cloud-like vanilla cream and kirsch-soaked cherries. An updated Black Forest gâteau in roulade form. There are several steps here so I'd treat this as an afternoon project, but it's an ideal crowd-pleaser for celebrations as it takes minutes to put together once the various components are made. Use the leftover cherry kirsch from the jar in cocktails or simmer it down to a thick syrup and spoon over the sliced roulade.

Serves 6–8
Preparation time: 1 hour, plus cooling
Cooking time: 25 minutes

For the chocolate ganache
100g (3½oz) dark chocolate (minimum 70% cocoa solids), finely chopped
100ml (3½fl oz/scant 1 cup) double (heavy) cream

For the flourless sponge
75g (2½oz) dark chocolate (minimum 70% cocoa solids), finely chopped
5 large free-range eggs, separated
a pinch of salt
175g (6oz/¾ cup) unrefined caster (superfine) sugar
3 tbsp cocoa (unsweetened chocolate) powder, sifted
1 tbsp ground almonds
200ml (7fl oz/scant 1 cup) double (heavy) cream
1 tbsp icing (confectioners') sugar, sifted
1 tsp vanilla bean paste
300g (10½oz) jar cherries in kirsch, drained and dried on paper towels
a handful of fresh cherries, to serve

To make the chocolate ganache, put the finely chopped chocolate in a heatproof bowl. Bring the cream up to boiling point in a small saucepan and pour over the chocolate, stirring once. Leave for a minute, then gently stir until shiny and smooth. Over-mixing will cause the ganache to split. Cover and chill until needed, making up to 48 hours ahead of time.

Preheat the oven to 160°C fan (180°C/350°F/gas 4). Neatly line the base and sides of a 33 × 23cm (13 × 9in) Swiss roll tin with a sheet of baking parchment.

To make the sponge, melt the chocolate in a bowl in the microwave, starting it off for 1 minute, then continuing in 20-second increments, stirring in between, until glossy and smooth. Alternatively, place in a heatproof bowl set above a saucepan of simmering water and warm through for a couple of minutes, stirring now and then until melted. Either way, set aside to cool.

Put the egg whites in a large bowl with the pinch of salt (this helps to break the egg whites down, enabling them to hold the air) and whisk until they hold stiff peaks.

In a separate bowl, whisk the egg yolks and caster sugar together on high speed for 2–3 minutes. The thick mixture should leave a ribbon-like trail when the beaters are lifted. Pour in the cooled chocolate and gently fold together until combined.

Gently stir 2 large spoonfuls of the egg whites into the chocolate mixture to loosen. Lightly fold in the remaining egg whites using a large metal spoon or spatula. The aim is to keep all the air in the batter so go gently in sweeping strokes. Sift 2 tablespoons of cocoa powder over the top and lightly fold it in with the ground almonds. Scrape into the prepared tin and smooth the top.

Bake for 20–25 minutes until risen and firm in the middle. Set aside to cool and deflate for a few minutes. Lay a large piece of non-stick baking parchment on a work surface. Turn the roulade out onto the paper so its lining paper is on top, then carefully peel off the paper. Fold a little of the base paper over one of the short sides and roll the roulade up to enclose the paper with it. Leave to cool completely. This will take around an hour.

Whip the cream, icing sugar and vanilla together until the cream thickens and holds its shape. Gently unroll the cooled roulade sponge on its paper. It is likely to crack a little, but don't worry. Spread the surface thinly with chocolate ganache, followed by the whipped cream mixture, leaving a border of about 2cm (¾in) all the way around the edges both times. Scatter with the well-dried cherries and roll up from the same short edge. Again, use the paper to help roll it as neatly and snugly as possible, but this time don't enclose any of it as you roll.

Roll the roulade so the join sits underneath, then transfer to a serving platter or board and sift the remaining cocoa powder over the top. Slice thickly and serve on delicate plates, accompanied with a few fresh cherries.

THE CARROT CAKE

Here it is: The Carrot Cake. Brown butter cream cheese frosting layered up with a pecan-studded spiced carrot sponge. Handsome, quietly fancy and fit for any celebration. No raisins in carrot cake on my watch, but feel free to add a handful to the batter if you love them.

Serves 10–12
Preparation time: 1 hour, plus cooling
Cooking time: 1 hour

**For the brown butter cream
cheese frosting**
140g (4½oz) unsalted butter, cubed
280g (10oz) full-fat cream cheese
140g (4½oz/heaped 1 cup) icing
   (confectioners') sugar, sifted
1 tsp vanilla bean paste
1 tsp lemon juice

For the carrot cake
240g (4½oz/scant 2 cups) self–raising
   flour
¼ tsp baking powder
1 tsp bicarbonate of soda (baking soda)
2 tsp ground cinnamon
1 tsp ground ginger
½ tsp fine sea salt
300g (10½oz/1⅔ cups) light soft
   brown sugar
250ml (9fl oz/1 cup) groundnut
   (peanut) or very mild olive oil
4 large free-range eggs
200g (7oz) carrots, trimmed and
   finely grated
100g (3½oz/1 cup) pecans, chopped
2 tsp vanilla extract or vanilla bean
   paste
4 rounds of stem ginger, finely
   chopped, plus 1 tbsp ginger syrup

To decorate
150g (5oz/1½ cups) pecan halves

To make the frosting, start by browning the butter at least an hour ahead of time. Once browned, the butter will keep covered in the fridge for several days so you can brown it well ahead and bring up to room temperature when needed. Add the cubed butter to a sturdy frying pan (skillet) set over a medium heat. Swirl the pan to melt it evenly and continue to cook, swirling regularly, for 4–5 minutes, or until it smells sweet and nutty and turns a light brown colour, flecked with golden milk solids. Transfer to a bowl and leave to cool and set for at least an hour.

To complete the frosting (again, it can be made about 3 days before icing the cake and kept covered in the fridge), drain the cream cheese in a sieve lined with a square of muslin or a clean tea (dish) towel. It will need about 20 minutes to drain the excess water away. Pick it up and give it a gentle squeeze in the fabric to rid it of as much moisture as possible then set aside.

Once the browned butter is at room temperature, use a wooden spoon and a large mixing bowl to beat the browned butter until fluffy. Add the sifted icing sugar and the vanilla extract, working them in gradually to make a thick paste with no dry areas. Now go in with the hand-held electric beaters, starting on a slow speed and whipping for about 4 minutes, gradually speeding up until you have a smooth and even, soft buttercream consistency. Add the drained cream cheese and the lemon juice and beat to just combine. The frosting should be a pale blonde colour, flecked with vanilla. Chill in the fridge for at least 30 minutes to further firm it up before using.

To make the cake, preheat the oven to 150°C fan (170°C/340°F/gas 3) and line the bases and sides of two 23cm (9in) round cake tins with non-stick baking parchment. Place the 150g (5oz) of pecan halves intended to decorate the cake on a baking sheet and toast in the oven for 10–12 minutes until golden and fragrant. Set aside to cool.

Sift the self-raising flour, baking powder, bicarbonate of soda, cinnamon and ginger into a large bowl, adding the salt as you do so. In another bowl, beat the brown sugar, oil and eggs together with a wooden spoon until smooth, then stir in the carrots, chopped pecans, vanilla extract, stem ginger and syrup. Pour the wet into the dry ingredients and combine with a spatula. Divide evenly between the tins and bake for about 35–40 minutes until risen and springy to the touch in the middle. Leave to cool in the tins for 5 minutes, then turn out to cool completely on a wire rack.

Stick your chosen base layer to a serving plate with a dab of the frosting. Using a palette knife or spatula, cover the top of this cake with a generous layer of frosting and sit the second cake over it, upside-down so that the top surface is as flat as possible. Cover the surface and sides thickly with frosting, using a palette knife or spatula to smooth and swoosh it evenly. I like to allow a little of the sponge to show through the frosting on the sides in places.

Crush or chop one-third of the toasted decoration pecans quite finely, saving the best halves to keep intact. Decorate the cake in retro style with the crushed pecans gently stuck to the cake around base and the remaining halves sitting around the edge on top.

SALTED HONEY CHEESECAKE POTS

I hope the restaurant Honey & Co. will forgive me for being inspired by their iconic feta cheesecake. All you need do to serve this is to layer the delectable salted cream cheese into glasses over a caramelised gingernut and smoked almond crumb. Spoon the fruit on top, drizzle with a thyme-honey syrup and finish with more of the addictive crumb. If you can't find thyme honey, another thick, dark and crystalline floral honey will do perfectly.

Serves 4
Preparation time: 40 minutes, plus cooling
Cooking time: 10 minutes

For the ginger crumbs
2 tbsp light soft brown sugar
30g (1oz/¼ cup) unsalted shelled pistachios
50g (1¾oz/¼ cup) smoked almonds
50g (1¾oz) gingernuts (ginger cookies), roughly crushed
50g (1¾oz) unsalted butter

For the syrup and cheesecake
150g (5oz) thyme honey
½ small orange, finely grated zest and 2 tbsp juice
1 vanilla pod (bean), split and seeds scraped out
2 tsp thyme leaves
100g (3½oz) best-quality feta, drained and crumbled
280g (9oz) full-fat cream cheese
250ml (9fl oz/1 cup) double (heavy) cream
75g (2½oz/scant ⅔ cup) icing (confectioners') sugar, sifted

To serve
4 ripe figs, quartered
4 tbsp pomegranate arials
1 tsp thyme leaves

To make the gingernut crumb, blitz the brown sugar, pistachios and smoked almonds together in a mini food processor until roughly chopped. Add the gingernuts and blitz again to make a rough crumb. You can, of course, do this by hand. Put the butter and these crumbs in a saucepan set over a low heat. Cook, stirring, for a few minutes until fragrant and golden, then set aside to cool completely. This can be made up to 4 days in advance and kept in an airtight container.

To make the honey syrup, put 75g (2½oz) of the honey in a small saucepan with the orange juice, scraped-out vanilla pod and thyme leaves. Heat through very gently for a few minutes to re-melt the honey and infuse it with vanilla and thyme. Set aside for 30 minutes to cool completely; it will thicken up as it does so. Strain before using if you want it to look refined; or just fish out the vanilla pod and leave the thyme leaves in. This can be made a few days ahead of time and kept cool until needed.

To make the cheesecake mixture, blitz the remaining honey with the feta, cream cheese, cream, icing sugar and reserved vanilla seeds together in a mini food processor or blender for a few seconds only until the feta is just smooth. Do not over-blend or the mixture will curdle. Better to have a few grains of feta remaining in the mix, so play it safe here. Fold in the grated orange zest to finish. This mixture can be covered and chilled for up to 72 hours.

To serve, use a generous hand to layer most of the crumb mixture – holding a little back – the feta mixture, figs, pomegranate arials and thyme leaves up in serving glasses. Spoon the honey syrup over the top – it should find its way down over the fruit and cream cheese layers – and finish with a little of the reserved smoked almond crumb.

ST CLEMENTS & ROSEMARY POSSETS
WITH ORANGE MACAROONS

Orange and lemon cream possets, scented with fresh rosemary and vanilla bean. Make them with blood oranges when in season – the possets will turn the palest pink – and set in little glasses or cups well in advance. You don't need to make the chewy orange zest-studded almond macaroons to go with, but they'll knock the socks off most bought biscuits.

Serves 6
Preparation time: 40 minutes, plus infusing and chilling
Cooking time: 25 minutes

For the macaroons
1 medium egg white
a pinch of salt
100g (3½oz/1 cup) ground almonds made from skin-on nuts
90g (3¼oz/heaped ⅓ cup) unrefined caster (superfine) sugar, plus extra to scatter over
2 tsp finely grated orange zest
16 whole, skin-on almonds, halved lengthways

For the possets
600ml (20fl oz/2½ cups) double (heavy) cream
1 wide strip of pared blood orange zest
2 rosemary sprigs
1 vanilla pod (bean), split
120g (4oz/½ cup) unrefined caster (superfine) sugar
150ml (5fl oz/scant ⅔ cup) fresh blood orange or orange juice
3 tbsp fresh lemon juice

To make the macaroons, beat the egg white and salt until almost forming soft peaks. There will be a little separated egg white at the base of the bowl. Combine the ground almonds, sugar and orange zest in a separate bowl. Fold in the egg whites, a tablespoon at a time, to make a thick, quite stiff batter.

Preheat the oven to 170°C fan (190°C/375°F/gas 5).

Roll the mix into small-walnut-sized balls and space out on a baking sheet, flattening the tops slightly. Top each with a halved almond (cut-side up), sprinkle with caster sugar to coat lightly, then let the macaroons sit for 15 minutes so that their tops dry out. Bake for 15–20 minutes until pale golden brown. The macaroons should still feel soft to the touch but they'll continue to harden as they cool. Leave on the baking sheet for at least 10 minutes before transferring to a cooling rack to cool completely.

To make the possets, start by putting the cream in a saucepan with the orange zest, rosemary and vanilla. Warm through over a low heat, without boiling, for 2 minutes, then cover and set aside to infuse for 20 minutes. Strain through a sieve to remove the orange zest, rosemary and vanilla, squeezing out the vanilla seeds from the pod directly into the cream (rinse and reuse the pod for other sweet things). Return the cream to a lowish heat with the sugar, stirring to dissolve, and bring almost to the boil. When just beginning to simmer, stir in the blood orange and lemon juices.

Divide between the glasses or cups and chill for at least 4 hours or overnight and serve with the biscuits.

RHUBARB, BUTTERMILK & CARDAMOM ICE CREAM

This is an exquisite and delicate ice cream intended to showcase tender stalks of pink forced or 'Champagne' rhubarb. You can make it without an ice cream machine, but it will be work. Clear a space in your freezer and pour the chilled ice cream base into a large mixing bowl. Freeze for a couple of hours until setting at the edges. Use a sturdy whisk to thoroughly whip any firm areas into the soft, making sure the mixture is smooth and as aerated as possible. Return to the freezer and repeat this process every hour until it is too thick to whip. Transfer to an ice cream container, cover and freeze for at least 4 hours or overnight until solid.

Serves 6 (makes 1.2 litres (40fl oz/4¾ cups) ice cream)
Preparation time: 30 minutes
Cooking time: 30 minutes
Freezing time: 4 hours minimum

For the compôte
550g (12lb 4oz) forced rhubarb, trimmed
50g (1¾oz) unrefined caster (superfine) sugar
6 green cardamom pods, bruised
juice of ½ lemon

For the ice cream
225g (8oz/scant 1 cup) unrefined caster (superfine) sugar
600ml (20fl oz/2½ cups) double (heavy) cream
300ml (10fl oz/1¼ cups) buttermilk
1 vanilla pod (bean), split and seeds scraped out
finely grated zest of ½ lemon

Preheat the oven to 160°C fan (180°C/350°F/gas 4).

Put the rhubarb in a ceramic baking dish or roasting tin large enough to contain it in a single layer. Scatter with the sugar and add the cardamom pods, lemon juice and 2 tablespoons of water. Cover with kitchen foil and roast in the middle of the oven for 25–30 minutes until the rhubarb is just soft but still holding its baton shapes. This will depend on its age; the younger and more tender the stalks, the less time they will take, so keep an eye after 20 minutes. Set the cooked rhubarb aside to cool, then remove the cardamom and return the seeds inside to the rhubarb, discarding the empty pods.

Use a slotted spoon to remove half the cooked rhubarb to a separate bowl. Chill the remaining rhubarb and juice as a compôte to go with the ice cream.

To make the ice cream, add the sugar, cream, buttermilk, vanilla seeds and lemon zest to the drained rhubarb. Whisk together using a balloon whisk. The rhubarb will break down as you whisk. Churn in the chilled bowl of an ice cream machine until the blades stop turning. Cover and freeze for at least 4 hours or overnight to set solid.

Serve the pale pink ice cream in scoops with the chilled compôte.

CHOCOLATE MOUSSE WITH BURNT SUGAR

This is an ingenious mousse, more of a ganache in truth, inspired, of course, by an even simpler Heston Blumenthal method of whipping chocolate and hot water together. I have tinkered with the idea and the proportions, balancing dark chocolate with sea salt, vanilla and maple syrup for a hint of sweetness without harming any vegan credentials. Serve it in a large dish with the shards of amber caramel, or divide between individual glasses or cups. The mousse is richly flavoured so small portions suffice, but the lack of cream or egg white makes it ethereally light to eat, with each spoonful delightfully melting away.

Serves 6
Preparation time: 20 minutes, plus cooling
Cooking time: 5 minutes
Vegan

For the mousse
300g (10½oz) dark chocolate (minimum 70% cocoa solids), finely chopped
1 tbsp maple syrup
a pinch of sea salt, plus extra flakes on top to serve
1 vanilla pod (bean), split and seeds scraped out

For the burnt sugar
150g (5oz/heaped ⅔ cup) granulated sugar

To make the burnt sugar shards, line a large baking sheet with a sheet of non-stick baking parchment. Put 2 tablespoons of water into a sturdy saucepan. Dredge the surface of the pan evenly with the sugar and place over a low–medium heat until the sugar starts to dissolve. Resist the temptation to stir the pan; only swirl as needed to keep the melting even. Once the sugar starts to dissolve, turn up the heat to medium–high and bubble down, swirling, until the sugar is an even and dark golden-brown.

Pour the caramel onto the paper in a thin, even layer. Leave to cool, then use a sharp knife to chop into smallish shards. Use right away or store in a tightly sealed container in a cool place for a few hours.

To make the chocolate mousse, half-fill a large bowl with ice and cover the ice with cold water. Place the chocolate in a second, smaller mixing bowl and add 275ml (9½fl oz/generous 1 cup) hot water from a recently boiled kettle. Using a whisk, mix until the chocolate has dissolved to make a watery chocolate-coloured liquid.

Place the chocolate bowl in the iced-water bath, making sure none of the icy water can spill into the inner bowl. Using hand-held electric beaters, whisk at high speed for a couple of minutes until the chocolate mixture begins to change form and thicken. It should still be shiny and loose.

Remove the bowl from the iced-water bath, add the maple syrup, salt and vanilla seeds and continue whisking until the mixture is just becoming softly set, like a gloopy, shiny ganache. Transfer to a serving bowl or individual cups before it over-thickens, smoothing the top. Cover and chill for at least 2 hours or up to 2 days until needed. Allow to sit at room temperature for 10 minutes before serving.

Serve the mousse with the caramel shards for scooping. You can also offer fresh raspberries and, if this pudding doesn't need to be vegan, chilled cream.

APPLE, AMARETTI & MARZIPAN CRUMBLE WITH AMARETTO CUSTARD

A crumble for almond aficionados, I'd make this in individual dishes for a dinner and in one large one for a supper, if that makes sense. The crumble mixture can be made a couple of days ahead and kept chilled until needed. You'll need about 4 cooking apples and 4 eating apples for this quantity, or you can double the quantities and keep on hand in the freezer for up to 3 months.

Serves 6
Preparation time: 20 minutes
Cooking time: 1 hour

200g (7oz/scant 1⅔ cups) plain (all-purpose) flour
50g (1¾oz/½ cup) ground almonds
1½ tsp ground cinnamon
¼ tsp fine salt
150g (5oz) unsalted butter, diced
100g (3½oz) marzipan (almond paste), diced into 1cm (½in) pieces
125g (4¼oz /⅔ cup) light muscovado sugar
50g (1¾oz) amaretti biscuits, roughly crumbled
50g (1¾oz/heaped ½ cup) flaked (slivered) almonds
800g (1lb 12oz) Bramley (cooking) apples, peeled, cored and roughly chopped (4 medium apples)
finely grated zest and juice of 1 lemon
600g (1lb 5oz) crisp eating (dessert) apples, peeled, quartered, cored and sliced

For the marzipan custard
500ml (17fl oz/2 cups) best-quality, bought fresh custard
50g (1¾oz) marzipan (almond paste), chopped
2 tbsp Amaretto
vanilla ice cream or Greek yogurt, to serve

Combine the flour, ground almonds, cinnamon and salt in a mixing bowl. Rub in the diced butter by hand until the mixture resembles coarse breadcrumbs. Rub in the marzipan, taking less care to break it down – some larger pieces can remain. Stir in 50g (1¾oz/heaped ¼ cup) of the muscovado sugar with the amaretti biscuits and lemon zest. Alternatively, pulse the flour and butter mixture together in the small bowl of a food processor, adding the sugar for a final few pulses once the mixture resembles coarse breadcrumbs and stirring in the marzipan, amaretti, flaked almonds and lemon zest at the end. Either way, cover and chill the crumble mix for 20 minutes or for up to 2 days (it also freezes well for up to 3 months).

Preheat the oven to 150°C fan (170°C/340°F/gas 3). Combine the apples with the lemon juice to prevent browning. Tumble in the remaining muscovado sugar, distributing the two apple types evenly. Transfer to a medium-sized baking dish that's about 23cm (9in) if round or about 20 × 25cm (8 × 10in) if not. Scatter the crumble over the fruit to cover completely.

Bake for about 1 hour 10 minutes until golden, crisp and bubbling at the edges.

To flavour the custard, put it in a blender with the 50g (1¾oz) of marzipan and the Amaretto. Blend for a couple of minutes (this needs to be thorough), then, if your blender isn't super-charged, pass through a sieve to remove any small marzipan pieces. The choice of very gently warmed through versus cold custard is up to you from this point.

Leave the crumble to settle for 10 minutes before serving with the marzipan custard and vanilla ice cream or with chilled Greek yogurt as a simpler option.

CHERRY GRANITA

The most elegant desserts are often the simplest. This is a granita to show off the deepest and juiciest late summer cherries, but you could certainly make it with frozen cherries or another ripe berry or stone fruit at its peak. Just be aware that too much sugar and too much alcohol will compromise the crystalline nature of the granita, potentially making it too smooth as it freezes, so err on the side of caution. Chilled pouring cream may seem an odd choice to accompany such fragile texture, but bear with me and try it. The combination of icy cherry with cool dairy is sublime.

Serves 8 generously
Preparation time: 20 minutes
Cooking time: 10 minutes,
plus 6 hours freezing

400g (14oz) pitted fresh cherries,
    plus 6 fresh cherries to decorate
½ vanilla pod (bean), split
150g (5oz/⅔ cup) unrefined caster
    (superfine) sugar
½ lemon, finely grated zest and juice
2 tbsp cherry brandy (optional)
300ml (10fl oz/1¼ cups) single
    (light) cream

Put the 400g of cherries into a large saucepan with 350ml (12¼fl oz/1½ cups) of water, the split vanilla pod half and the sugar. Place over a low heat, bring to a simmer and cook gently for 10–15 minutes until the cherries have softened completely.

Remove the vanilla pod, then tip the mixture into a blender with the lemon zest and juice. Blend thoroughly until smooth, then push the mixture through a fine sieve, using the back of a spoon to force as much liquid through as possible. Stir in the cherry brandy, if using, but don't be tempted to add more as it will prevent the granita from freezing solid.

Pour into a large baking dish or roasting tin that will sit flat in your freezer and freeze for an hour. Use a fork to scrape the frozen edges into the middle, then freeze again. The timings will depend slightly on the size of the dish you've used but repeat this scraping process 3–4 times at hourly intervals until the granita has formed icy crystals throughout and can be left to freeze for at least 2 more hours before serving. Ideally you'd leave it overnight. Give it a last scrape to separate, then spoon the purple granita into delicate, chilled glasses to serve with a flood of chilled cream and a fresh cherry garnish.

PEACH & HAZELNUT FRANGIPANE TART

A patisserie-worthy tart, heady with peaches, buttery hazelnut frangipane and hints of vanilla. You'll need a 23cm (9in) diameter, 6cm (2½in) deep tart tin with a removable base to make this tart, plus about 500g (1lb 2oz) of baking beans, raw pulses or uncooked rice for the blind baking step. If you can't find whole hazelnuts with skins on, blanched will be fine, just miss out the skinning step after roasting.

Serves 8
Preparation time: 20 minutes, plus 30 minutes chilling
Cooking time: 1 hour 15 minutes

500g (1lb 2oz) all-butter, shortcrust pastry, chilled

2 tsp plain (all-purpose) flour, plus extra for rolling the pastry if needed

150g (5oz/heaped 1 cup) whole hazelnuts, preferably with skins

150g (5oz) unsalted butter, softened

150g (5oz/⅔ cup) unrefined caster (superfine) sugar

2 tsp vanilla bean paste

2 small eggs, beaten

4 tbsp apricot jam

6 large, ripe peaches, pitted and quartered

1 tbsp icing (confectioners') sugar, sifted

crème fraîche or similar, to serve

Roll the chilled pastry out to a circle about 27cm (10¾in) in diameter and 5mm (¼in) thick using a little plain (all-purpose) flour to prevent it sticking, if necessary. Pick the pastry up by rolling gently over your rolling pin and drape it into a 6cm (2½in) deep, 23cm (9in) tart tin with a removable base. Carefully press the pastry in with your fingertips, leaving the edges overhanging, and prick the base all over with a fork. Chill for at least 30 minutes.

Preheat the oven to 160°C fan (180°C/350°F/gas 4) when ready to bake the pastry.

Put the hazelnuts on a baking sheet and roast for 8 minutes or so until pale golden and fragrant. The papery skins should have turned darker and be peeling away. Tip the hot hazelnuts into a clean tea (dish) towel, bring the edges up to enclose them and rub vigorously to remove as many of the skins as possible. This doesn't have to be a perfect job. Transfer the roast nuts to a bowl and leave to cool. If you could only find blanched hazelnuts, obviously miss out this skinning step.

Place a large sheet of non-stick baking parchment on top of the pastry and fill the middle with baking beans, raw pulses or uncooked rice to weigh the pastry down and keep it in place. Bake for 20 minutes then carefully remove the paper containing the beans. Continue to cook the uncovered tart for about 10 minutes more until pale golden and sandy-looking. Trim the excess edges flush with the tin using a sharp knife (I find serrated best). The cooked case can be kept in a sealed container in a cool place for a few days at this stage, if needed.

To make the frangipane, place the roast hazelnuts in a food processor and blend to grind quite finely, being careful not to over-blend or they may become oily. Some texture is fine. In a mixing bowl, beat the soft butter and the sugar together with a wooden spoon for 2 minutes until fluffy. Add the ground hazelnuts, 2 tsp flour and the vanilla, beating briefly until evenly combined. Beat in the eggs to finish. If convenient, cover and chill the mixture for an hour or overnight, but it is fine to move straight on with the recipe.

Make sure the oven is turned or preheated to 150°C fan (170°C/340°F/gas 3). Spread the apricot jam evenly over the base of the blind-baked pastry case.

Spoon the frangipane over the jam layer somewhat evenly, nestle the peach slices on top in concentric circles and bake for about 40 minutes, or until the frangipane is golden, risen and firm. It will have encased some of the peaches. Leave to rest for 15 minutes and dust with icing sugar before removing from the tin, serving slices warm or at room temperature with crème fraîche on the side.

PORTUGUESE CARAMELISED ALMOND TART

This is not so much a tart as an upside-down caramel almond cake. You'll find many of these almond tarts in Portugal, but they can vary enormously and, upon asking in the kitchens of restaurants serving good ones, I found the chefs' recipes to be … elusive. This is an amalgamation and imagination of every excellent version I've tried, balanced with salt to counter the caramel. You'll need to track down 'nibbed' or slivered almonds: blanched almonds that have been cut into tiny match-stick shapes. Find them online or in health food stores.

Serves 8
Preparation time: 15 minutes
Cooking time: 45–50 minutes

For the salted caramel layer
75g (2½oz) slightly salted butter
75g (2½oz/⅓ cup) unrefined caster (superfine) sugar
5 tbsp double (heavy) cream
1 vanilla pod (bean), split open and seeds scraped out
a pinch of sea salt flakes

For the caramel almond layer
150g (5oz/⅔ cup) unrefined caster (superfine) sugar
100g (3½oz) slightly salted butter
100ml (3½fl oz/scant ½ cup) whole milk
200g (7oz/heaped 1¼ cups) nibbed almonds

For the sponge layer
120g (4oz) slightly salted butter, softened
120g (4oz/heaped ½ cup) unrefined caster (superfine) sugar
2 large eggs
100g (3½oz/heaped ¾ cup) self-raising flour
20g (¾oz/scant ¼ cup) ground almonds
2 tbsp whole milk
1 tbsp icing (confectioners') sugar, sifted

vanilla ice cream or crème fraîche, to serve

Preheat the oven to 160°C fan (180°C/350°F/gas 4). Butter the insides of a deep 25cm (10in) round cake tin with a removable base. Line the base and sides with non-stick baking parchment.

To make the salted caramel layer, put the sugar in a heavy-based pan and set over a low heat. Swirl the pan as the sugar begins to melt and turn golden, ensuring the syrup colours evenly. Once the caramel is a uniform amber colour, add the butter, cream, scraped vanilla seeds and scrunched salt, stirring to melt the butter and make a smooth caramel. Remove from the heat and set aside.

Preferably using an electric mixer or hand-held beaters, beat the softened butter and sugar together for 2 minutes until thick and fluffy. Add the eggs while still beating, one by one, and continue to beat for a further minute, then add the flour and ground almonds, beating on a low speed just until combined. Add the milk and combine briefly, then spoon a scant three-quarters of the mixture into the tin. Spread with the salted caramel – in reality this will mean covering as much of the surface as possible with half-teaspoonfuls of caramel and smoothing these out a little. Cover the caramel with the remaining cake batter, smoothing the top so that no caramel shows through.

Bake for about 20 minutes until risen and golden. A skewer inserted into the middle of the cake should come out with no wet batter sticking to it.

Meanwhile, make the almond topping so it's ready to go by the time the cake is cooked. Place the sugar, butter and milk in a saucepan over a gentle heat, stirring until the butter melts. Turn up the heat to medium–high and continue to cook for a few minutes, stirring occasionally until boiling and like pale, molten toffee in colour and consistency. Stir in the almonds and remove from the from heat.

Pour the hot almond mixture over the cooked cake, using a spatula to spread the almonds out to cover the top evenly. Bake for 20 minutes, or until the almond caramel is dark golden at the edges. Leave to sit for 20 minutes to firm up, then carefully transfer to a cooling rack, almond-side up. Dust lightly with icing sugar and serve warm or at room temperature with ice cream or crème fraîche.

BAKED RUM PINEAPPLE WITH SWEET SPICES

Rum, pineapple, fragrant spices in caramel ... this is kitsch. Make it less so by lopping off the leafy crown before cooking; the resulting burnished pineapple will be more grown-up. Serve in warm slices with chilled crème fraîche or vanilla ice cream to melt into the sauce.

Serves 4
Preparation time: 15 minutes
Cooking time: 1 hour

1 large, ripe pineapple
150g (5oz/heaped ¾ cup) light muscovado sugar
1 vanilla pod (bean), split and seeds scraped out
5 green cardamom pods, bruised
2 whole star anise
1 cinnamon stick, broken in half
200ml (7fl oz/scant 1 cup) spiced dark rum
50g (1¾oz) salted butter, diced
crème fraîche or vanilla ice cream, to serve

Preheat the oven to 170°C fan (190°C/375°F/gas 5).

To prepare the pineapple, remove the base and the peel with a sharp knife, revealing the yellow flesh. Remove the 'eyes' left behind; the most efficient way is to cut them out in rows by slicing thin diagonal wedges away around the surface of the fruit. It's your choice whether or not to leave the leafy crown in place for baking; lopping it off is perhaps the more modern option.

Put the sugar, split vanilla pod and scraped-out seeds, cardamom pods, star anise, broken cinnamon stick, rum and butter in a small saucepan. Bring slowly to the boil, stirring to melt the butter, and simmer gently for a couple of minutes until smooth. Place the pineapple on its side in a medium-sized baking dish and cover with the sauce, rotating it to coat.

Roast in the middle of the oven for 50–55 minutes, turning every 10 minutes and spooning the sauce over to baste when you do so.

Towards the end of the cooking time, the caramel may begin to catch at the edges. If it does, stir in a splash of water. Once the pineapple is caramelised and tender, remove from the oven and leave it to cool for 15 minutes before slicing at the table and serving with your choice of crème fraîche or ice cream and the caramel sauce from the dish.

SEASONAL MENU PLANS

Here are some recipe combinations for various occasions. They are arranged seasonally to help you make best use of ingredients when they are at their most characterful and abundant. I've kept an eye on complementary styles, textures and flavours throughout each menu and the make-ahead notes are particularly useful in helping you to take the stress out of entertaining. You'll notice any sweet course is either made completely in advance, or ready to put together when needed with very little fuss; a key trick to enable the host to relax and enjoy themselves when cooking for others, I feel. I hope they will also inspire you with the confidence to be more adventurous in your own combinations and in adapting recipes to suit your own preferences, the ingredients available and the time you have at your disposal.

RELAXED
SPRING BRUNCH

The Ultimate Avocado Toast (page 18)

Lentil & Spinach Shakshuka (page 47)

Salted Honey Cheesecake Pots (page 200)

MAKE-AHEAD NOTES

A few days ahead (unless you are using ready-made relishes):
Make the pink pickles for the toasts.
Make the chilli oil for the toasts and the shakshuka.
Make the piri piri sauce for the shakshuka.

Two days ahead
Make all the component parts for the cheesecake pots and keep the crumbs
and the thyme honey covered and the cheesecake mixture chilled.

A day ahead
Make the shakshuka base and keep chilled.
Make the smoky beans for the avocado toasts and keep chilled.

When ready to serve
Assemble and finish the dishes as written, reheating the beans and the
shakshuka base to cook the eggs.

MAKE-AHEAD
SUMMER DINNER

Slow-Cooked Courgettes with Salted Ricotta & Pine Nuts (page 150) served on focaccia toasts

Baked Stuffed Tomatoes with Saffron, Fennel & Lentil Rice (page 122) served with a green leaf salad dressed with Grain Mustard Vinaigrette (page 175)

Peach & Hazelnut Frangipane Tart (page 212)

MAKE-AHEAD NOTES

A few days ahead (unless you are using ready-made relishes)

Make the chilli pepper relish for the courgettes
and keep chilled.

Make the rouille for the tomatoes and keep covered
and chilled.

Make the mustard vinaigrette for the tomatoes
and keep chilled.

Two days ahead

Make the slow-cooked courgettes and keep covered and chilled.

A day ahead

Make the tart and keep it covered in a cool larder or in the fridge.

When ready to serve

Assemble and finish the dishes as written, serving the courgettes, the baked
tomatoes and the tart at room temperature or reheating very gently.

WINTER SUPPER

Twice-Roast Beetroot in a Fig & Watercress Salad (page 139)

Risotto with Roast Radicchio & Black Olive Crumb (page 94) with Baked Red Onion Petals with Grain Mustard Vinaigrette (page 156)

Rhubarb, Buttermilk & Cardamom Ice Cream (page 205)

MAKE-AHEAD NOTES

Three days ahead
Make the vinaigrette for the onions and keep chilled.
Make the ice cream and keep in the freezer.
Make the compôte and keep chilled.

Two days ahead
Cook the beetroots and keep chilled.
Make the dressing for the salad and keep chilled.
Make the black olive crumb for the risotto and keep covered in a cool place.

A day ahead
Make the red onion petals and keep chilled.

Earlier in the day
Chop the onions for the risotto.
Prepare the radicchio in a roasting tin and keep chilled.

When ready to serve
Assemble and finish the dishes as written, gently reheating the onion petals.
Consider folding rocket leaves through the red onions to make more of a
salad to accompany the risotto.

RELAXED VEGAN AUTUMN DINNER

Five-Spice Spring Rolls (page 82) with Pickled Carrots (page 182)
using the vegan black rice vinegar dip for the spring rolls

Mushroom, Pumpkin & Chestnut Claypot (page 110)
served with steamed brown rice and stir-fried or steamed greens

Chocolate Mousse with Burnt Sugar (page 206)

MAKE-AHEAD NOTES

Three days ahead (unless you are using ready-made relishes and oil)
Make the spring roll filling and keep covered and chilled.
Make the pickled carrots.
Make the fragrant chilli oil (up to a couple of weeks ahead).

Two days ahead
Make the black rice vinegar dip for the rolls and keep chilled.
Make the claypot and keep chilled.
Make the chocolate mousse and keep chilled.

A day ahead
Make the burnt sugar and keep covered in a cool place.

Two hours ahead
Fill and fry the spring rolls.

When ready to serve
Assemble and finish the dishes as written, reheating the spring rolls well-spaced out on baking sheets in a moderate oven until crisp, thoroughly reheating the claypot and steaming brown rice and greens to accompany.

INDEX

ABOUT THE AUTHOR

Alice Hart is an established and experienced London-based food writer, food stylist, chef and nutritionist (MSc). Her vibrant, seasonal vegetarian recipes celebrate wholefoods, spices and herbs by the handful, as well as vegetables themselves. Formerly the food editor of *Waitrose Food Illustrated Magazine*, Alice has been a regular contributor to *The New York Times*, *The Times*, *The Sunday Times*, the *Guardian*, the *Observer* and the *Telegraph*. *Repertoire* is Alice's fourth vegetarian cook book of many and her second cookbook for Welbeck, following their publication of *The Magnificent Book of Vegetables* in 2022.

ACKNOWLEDGEMENTS

Thank you to Kate Pollard at Welbeck for commissioning these two vegetable-packed books with characteristic style, vision, expertise, guidance and enthusiasm. Daniel New brought the cover to life and brought his talent and style to every one of these pages, translating words and pictures into a book to treasure. Thank you to editor Wendy Hobson for tireless and exacting work on the copy and recipes, making sure we have been clear for the reader as well as inspiring them. Claudia Young at Greene and Heaton, thank you. Thanks also to the rest of the Welbeck team for getting this book published.

Emma, thank you for your creativity, inspired styling, sensational photography and use of your studio space (above and beyond). Thank you, Indi, for your incredible hard work with Emma, impromptu hand modelling and enthusiasm. Sadie Albuquerque was also a pivotal part of the photography process and a joyful presence, helping me with recipe testing as well as being an essential help with the food styling. Eleanor at Pearson Lyle, thank you for sorting everything with your typical grace and efficiency.

It is all so appreciated.

To dear friends and family who are always enthusiastic about my books and better at PR than me.

Lastly, thank you to James, my love, whom I adore cooking with most of all.

Published in 2023 by OH Editions,
part of Welbeck Publishing Group.
Offices in: London – 20 Mortimer Street, London W1T 3JW &
Sydney – Level 17, 207 Kent St, Sydney NSW 2000, Australia
www.welbeckpublishing.com

Design and layout © 2023 Welbeck Non-Fiction Ltd
Text copyright © 2023 Alice Hart
Photography © 2023 Emma Lee
Illustrations © 2023 Daniel New

A CIP catalogue record for this book is available from the British Library.

ISBN 978-1-80453-076-4

Publisher: Kate Pollard
Desk editor: Matt Tomlinson
Designer and illustrator: Daniel New
Copy editor: Wendy Hobson
Food stylist: Alice Hart
Food stylist's assistant: Sadie Albuquerque
Photography and prop styling: Emma Lee
Photography assistant: Indiana Petrucci
Production controller: Arlene Alexander
Colour reproduction: p2d

Printed and bound by Leo in China

10 9 8 7 6 5 4 3 2 1